INSIDE THE EARTHQUAKE PALACE

INSIDE THE EARTHQUAKE PALACE

4

PLAYS

WILL ALEXANDER

CHAX
2011

ISBN 978 0925904 89 8

Published by Chax Press
411 N 7th Ave Ste 103
Tucson, Arizona 85705-8388
USA

Printed in the United States of America

*"... my characters ... burn
the curtain and die in the
presence of the public"*

— Garcia Lorca

CONDUCTION IN THE CATACOMBS

A Play in Three Acts

Characters:
CORTAENIA, Mexican, American born, 28, full-figured, sand-blind.

EURYDICE, Brazilian and Jewish, brought to West Texas at birth, of a lean but womanly build, about 32 years old.

Place:
An isolate mental sanitarium in West Texas

Time:
The anonymous present

ACT ONE

A darkened enclave, the walls colored with a dark institutional green paint, a worn sofa-like chair at the center of the state, facing the audience, slightly shifted at an angle stage left. At the back of the stage, stage right, a smoke darkened wall heater. There is a susurrant singing which silences when the darkness transmutes into a white diffuse light. CORTAENIA sits, hunched forward in the chair, tense, in a besmirched institutional dressing gown, partially blind, in darkened glasses, wearing old, worn house slippers, her seeing-eye cane poised against the audience side of char. She is being maniacally circled by EURYDICE, herself in a stained institutional dressing gown, barefoot, her left arm dangling, bandaged from the wrist to the top of the forearm. As the action commences, EURYDICE directly parallel to CORTAENIA, continuing to speak without breaking her movement.

EURYDICE. You connive, you always verbally connive, Cortaenia. You know what I've been through, you know I've been condemned to live at this pitch, that I've forcibly been brutalized.

CORTAENIA. *A strange diplomacy in her voice.* But you know it's been the same for me, Eurydice, lingering in this cold imbalance, burst, and sown together again with seeds. Look, we've been doused with alienation and thrown together in this dungeon as two culpable dice.

EURYDICE. *Circling furiously, her voice almost violent.* What do you mean? Phantoms?

CORTAENIA. *With heightened voice.* They've abandoned us, Eurydice; they've shut away our shadows, our empty diagrams, our fractured bodies. Are we fed or soaped with any kind of alacrity? Are we respected as being part of the properly living? Look at how your arm suppurates with infection. Listen to the way my eyes hiss, the way

10

my throat improperly parches.

EURYDICE. *Intense heightened voice.* You know, sometimes my arm feels green, disrupted, paralyzed.

CORTAENIA. I can never see us leaving here alive, Eurydice. I can only feel the murderer's nostrums, the summoned vulture's priorities.

EURYDICE. My mother always told me that my blood would be abandoned, that the crops would fail in my voice, that the wood of my body would flood away and contaminate.
Erratically stops circling. Almost spouting staccato.
She told me I was infected within a poisoned copulator's prism, that I was spawned in aboriginal night salts, that I was a strange transparent sexual beast.

CORTAENIA. So you blame yourself, Eurydice?

EURYDICE. I only know that the brutality seems stronger, that the cold inside me bleeds and leaves suffering like a swan, constantly hatched from piranhas.

CORTAENIA. You see, we're not needed, Eurydice, we're feathers, we're despicable mushroom burns.

Pause.

I know that I'm legally blind, but I've figured out the alphabet and I know that Lorca existed. But what keeps me alive is that I can always call on a sudden strangeness of speech.

EURYDICE. *Starting to circle again.* So you know writing, you know its warring linguistics.

CORTAENIA. Early on, my sister would condescendingly read plays to me. It was like a gloating in her voice about my blindness. She would irregularly read aloud Lorca's *Bernarda Alba*. And she would almost become Bernarda, her ethos momentarily stung beneath a fiery delta of guilt. To her, being the younger I was already the prototype of the mournful Angustias, mumbling like a table of slain sparrows, under the watchful cruelty of eagles. But she would always cover her stains by saying that she was taking me to great heights, that she was blessing me with grace.

EURYDICE. What do you mean, grace, the great heights?

CORTAENIA. The explosions, Eurydice, the verbal lightning conveyed through Lorca.

EURYDICE. You mean a ring of literary fossils.

CORTAENIA. *Agitated.* No!

EURYDICE. *Continuing to circle.* How could I ever lead someone like you, wrought by all your rancid solar hatreds?

CORTAENIA. You're baiting me, Eurydice. What do you want me to say? That I'm a shellfish, an imposter?

EURYDICE. Look, you're branded, you hate that you're blinded, and so you accuse me of calling you an adder.
CORTAENIA. Stop circling me, Eurydice!

EURYDICE. So you can see.

CORTAENIA. I'm sand-blind, I'm simply sand-blind.

EURYDICE. *Cuttingly.* Your nerves are red.

CORTAENIA. Because I can't sculpt the image of a lamp or optically ignite a tree…

EURYDICE. You're asking me for mercy. Am I God? Do you want me to be your sister's replacement?

CORTAENIA. *Her voice smoldering.* You're evil, Eurydice. You slashed your arm, you wanted death.

EURYDICE. You accuse me, and all you spout is a blackened mathematics. It's like a blunted cortical drill.

CORTAENIA. You can see, Eurydice, but you've never known beauty. Only hair, dust, sweat, pollution.

EURYDICE. So I'm compounded. And if I wanted death, I wanted death!

CORTAENIA. All I know is that you've ruined your own shadow and you feel to me like apparitional Braille.

EURYDICE. *Insidiously.* So you're the blind sun and I'm the poisoned planet.

CORTAENIA. Astronomy, the Pleiades. You've bled, Eurydice, your arm has an odor.

EURYDICE. You're just jealous because your life is so arrested. The heat you inspire is like charcoal or pain.

CORTAENIA. Of course, I'm bizarre. I've been obstructed. I was once seventeen and mature.

EURYDICE. I can only say that your humor is bloody and your night

13

sweats inspire motionless calamity.

Pause

A touch of contriteness in her voice. Perhaps we don't exist, perhaps we're polemical apparitions and I'm forced to circle your star for eternity.

CORTAENIA. How can you tell me I don't thrive, that my lust has ceased, that I've vanished through the hearts of volcanoes?

EURYDICE. *With heightened voice.* You admitted we don't exist and that we'll die and live here forever.

CORTAENIA. Old deposed nuns.

EURYDICE. Yes, old deposed nuns.

CORTAENIA. If I could properly see, I'd obtain a mirror from Heliopolis and see remnants of flesh scattered across a smoking poltergeist's stage.

EURYDICE. An eclipse body.

CORTAENIA. Yes, an eclipse body.

EURYDICE. Cortaenia, between us we have three arms, two clear eyes, with mingled phantoms between us.

CORTAENIA. The demons have blessed me with poise and I'll blindly sew my death suit. And the State will come and color its force with standard inequity and error.

EURYDICE. What's absurd, Cortaenia, is that I know we're random

14

kindling, we're carnivorous Pandoras, doubled over in drowning.

CORTAENIA. On a calendar I'll write that we're spores from Armageddon. That we're thirsting tourmaline angels.

EURYDICE. When I lost the use of my arm, my eyes faltered, my speech was impaired, my sex was disrupted.

CORTAENIA. You're giving me codes.

EURYDICE. No, Cortaenia, I'm not giving you codes!

CORTAENIA. Then you're implying that my eyes are unclouded, that I retransmit my failures, that I burn up my instants in shadows.

EURYDICE. How can I rival you, how can I prejudice any delivery you may offer? I'm only this way because I scalded my father in his sleep and produced a surge of blisters around his colon. Why? Because I was angry, because the juices were black in my marrow.

CORTAENIA. So why do you always imply that you'll escape me, that you'll take away the fact of the galaxy from my face? I've carried the same stumbling auras, you with paralysis, I with my blindness.

EURYDICE. Cortaenia, I'll say it like this. We have respective oblivions. As for my condition, I know my mother took a viper's drug and psychically kidnapped demons and made sixty-four hours of love with an incubus. This I know, without cursing, without the shell of my loins being rapid with anger.

CORTAENIA. *With disgust.* You're acidic, Eurydice.

EURYDICE. Because you're blind. All you can hear is my tropical bladder, my spine, my realms of leper's fury.

15

CORTAENIA. *Accusatory.* So you blame your mother. You accuse her of some distorted ovarian crime.

EURYDICE. *Rapidly.* It was my father, him the incubus. He convinced her through hours of love, and that after I was born I'd have a half-life between three and six months' duration.

CORTAENIA. It makes no sense, Eurydice.

Eurydice. They originally came from Paraguay and they'd just as soon drink your blood. Look, their emotions were spoiled and wrongly pillaged from speech.

CORTAENIA. So you lied about being born in Sao Paulo.

EURYDICE. No, I have all my dates correct. How could I remember, confused and given a death strike at birth?

CORTAENIA. So you grew up wild in Amarillo.

> *Pause*

Me, I'm originally from Magdalena, so I'm originally New Mexican. It's a difference.

EURYDICE. *Continuing to circle.* So where did you first make love? In Magdalena or San Angelo?

CORTAENIA. What difference does it make!

EURYDICE. *Almost shouting.* It's where you were spawned, it's where your birth developed. It's where...

CORTAENIA. So you want to correct me, you want to tear off pieces

16

of light and make ravens in your sleep?

EURYDICE. Now, you've admitted that I've taken your power and that I'm standing on thresholds.

CORTAENIA. All you've done is turn my name around with your lies. It's like listening to my mother burn as I progressed to this depth in my blindness. I keep hearing in your sound this monotonous faucet of nausea. This wayward ambling at my throat.

EURYDICE. You can't stop me from speaking. These examples do exist. You can't know this because you only listen. I gesticulate with my glances.

CORTAENIA. *Angered.* All you do is patronize with those worthless husks in your throat.

EURYDICE. Look, we're forced to live in this sealess deficit, this...

CORTAENIA. *Smoldering.* You patronize and you lie.

EURYDICE. Look at you, no morals, pontificating.
    With bitterness.
You'd even poach carrion.

CORTAENIA. No, Quetzalcoatl has already condemned you.

EURYDICE. *Stops her circling and stands in front of* CORTAENIA.
All you have to do is stare at me and you can see the truth.

    Pause.

What are you waiting for? You won't look, I don't even see you breathing.

17

CORTAENIA. *Loudly.* Mockery!

EURYDICE. No, you just want a paradigm, an acidic methodology, a vacantly squared voltage.

CORTAENIA. So, I'm nothing but a vacant thorn, some emblematic residue?

EURYDICE. You've reaped the things you can't see.

> *Partially pulling up her gown.*

The marks on my thighs—to you they're nothing but voids, disabled sociologies.

CORTAENIA. what do you want me to do, hand paint your rape? Color your throat with Roman make-up and blood?

EURYDICE. *Resuming her circling of* CORTAENIA. I'm neither commanding nor judging. I'm simply stating facts.

CORTAENIA. What have you ever known except that old incubus lying in your bed? I can sense that your body still burns that way.

EURYDICE. You speak of me, yet you, you, intoxicated with filth, with that lava you suppress inside your forehead…

CORTAENIA. You rotten piece of…

EURYDICE. I attempted to sever my arteries, I'll admit that. I took advantage of my horror, I farmed my own insolvency.

CORTAENIA. Why didn't you just scream and break up the dark with your thinking. I would always take a wooden clause out of smoke and violently break it with water.

EURYDICE. Nothing would help except to tear up my body.

More agitated in her circling, her voice practically at a pitch.

You've never wanted your blindness dissolved, to have your blindness go away!

CORTAENIA. I've always seen my abilities as a way of igniting my instants. During the daylight I would draw a sand and rose cathedral over and over, so I expanded my puberty, I…

EURYDICE. What you're telling me is that you couldn't properly stand on your own.

CORTAENIA. How could I accuse my own family?

EURYDICE. Accuse them, just accuse them.

CORTAENIA. Stop trying me.

EURYDICE. You're not speaking.

CORTAENIA. You want me to say I was his. That my mother only bickered to keep from hurting. That my sister was starved and raped.

EURYDICE. So you can feel how it builds, how the tedium eats away and protracts in the soul.

CORTAENIA. So your arm went numb.

EURYDICE. Yes, my arm is numb and it's listless and necrotic. Twenty-three months, Cortaenia, and it's still necrotic. It's been so bad that I'd randomly stain the china out of spite. I've been told the nerves have disappeared, that the blood has dried up.

19

CORTAENIA. Are you saying that we agree on dementia, on the way they observe us?

EURYDICE. Good, you are sand-blind.

CORTAENIA. My mother would accuse me of vanity, of being a carnivore. She said that I tried to exist above the wrath of human worth and I failed.

EURYDICE. And you're agreeing?

CORTAENIA. No, it's been my life. I've been witness to constant frailty.

ACT TWO

As in Act One, the singing sussurates and goes silent as the darkened stage brightens. EURYDICE *continues to circle the abstract sun of* CORTAENIA.

EURYDICE. Cortaenia, pretend we're wolves under a bolt of purple lightning willows. Pretend your sorcery extended through space and bled through the locality of Andromeda. Pretend you've transferred souls in their graves. Pretend you've died and changed the weather in your star group.

CORTAENIA. Circulation.

EURYDICE. Yes, circulation. If the Sun has failed us, why not we fail the Sun.

CORTAENIA. It's try, I can't contend with the galaxy. It disturbs me, it gives me chills like wearing an eerie serpent's leather.

EURYDICE. But it's happening, Cortaenia. The words are already bleeding. You're mentally drizzling scorpions. Tell me how it feels, how the blood mentally drizzles in your brain.

CORTAENIA. So you admit that your arm is blind, that you've suffered a half act of suicide.

EURYDICE. It makes me go blank and chatter.

CORTAENIA. Horrible terminologies like ruthless canine invictas. It seems that all you want to do is shut off the sun and vainly block out the light.

EURYDICE. Now you sound like a young madam in bondage. It seems like a paradox of leakage and anti-hurtling maneuver.

CORTAENIA. So I'm the blinded tree, the spark that decimates, which profoundly confuses.

EURYDICE. Take your mother. I'm sure she feels justified in having you rot here, without taking off your clothes, year after insidious year in blankness. She somehow blames you, wants to sculpt you to her own desire of damage.

CORTAENIA. All I know is that she would encourage him while the rest of the family would stare and I'd take on the role of the mother.

EURYDICE. Take ore...

CORTAENIA. *Incredulously.* So you're suggesting my eyes are ore.

EURYDICE. For instance, alabaster moons.

CORTAENIA. Divine justification?

EURYDICE. Think this way: perhaps we are eating point by point into the murderous flanks of God. Perhaps, within a corrupted Chinese arc, we have found balance by burning the outer symmetrical poles.

CORTAENIA. So you cease to hover at the Occident.

EURYDICE. *Somewhat joyfully.* At provable data. How can we possibly halt at any provable biology?

CORTAENIA. *Agreeing.* Yes! It's like going beyond a rumor or a whisper in a poisoned bloodbath.

EURYDICE. This is how they infect us, divide us.

CORTAENIA. Through the corporeal.

EURYDICE. Yes, through the corporeal.

CORTAENIA. Not making you violent. I have ceased to divide you, or make absurdities, as though my powers could legislate comets.

EURYDICE. But you have this evil about you, Cortaenia, this brine…

CORTAENIA. *Emphatically.* Nothing is ever alike.

EURYDICE. You want to create divergence, to implement implosion, to build a syllabus of wrath, by which you project an alien integer, which staggers.

CORTAENIA. *Disdainfully.* You're just creating confusion. Worthless episodes…

EURYDICE. I have nothing against you, Cortaenia. Perhaps if my eyes…

CORTAENIA. *Angered.* My eyes again, all you want to do is talk about my eyes.

EURYDICE. You're just bitter.

CORTAENIA. No, it's you who connives. Even when you slashed yourself you connived. Because you're weak you constructed the blood from your wound like a shield.

EURYDICE. Maybe I wanted to experiment with death.

   More heatedly.

I'm a pathfinder. In three thousand years, there will be less death and less vapor. And, you know, three thousand years is nothing. It is only a means, a path. You know the fornication of starlight. If I gave you a billion-plus years to coagulate, what would it mean if you genuinely sought to float between galaxies? What would helium mean? How would the zone of New Mexico remain prudent?

CORTAENIA. I'm only asking that you leave my eyes alone, that you stop this maniacal circling around the snow line.

EURYDICE. So how do you want to be dealt with? As utopian, as beggar?

CORTAENIA. I've gone a lot higher than those levels.

Insistent.

Why do you demean me, why do you try so hard to demean me?

EURYDICE. I've tried nothing, Cortaenia. Do you think your position creates envy?

CORTAENIA. Yet you yourself admit that you'll circle my sun for all time.

EURYDICE. No, I'm only circling grass in a doll's vacuum.

CORTAENIA. Again you mislead. I am in line with the Mayan stela at Quiriguá sweeping back "400,000,000" years into the vapor. I can affix counts and tables and different cyclical series. I conduct my central computations from maize, when the age of the Sun was beginning.

EURYDICE. *Somewhat negatively.* Such grandiloquence, Cortaenia. Yet I feel punished from so much burning.

CORTAENIA. For the sum of your presence I affix its ether in uinals or days. As for me, I am the center of vigesimal zeros.

EURYDICE. Then you want the sum to break my blood, to tear open soils in my carbon.

CORTAENIA. I made no such reference.

EURYDICE. As if my darkness were hand-sown.

CORTAENIA. Eurydice, listen: the authorities have no other cause than having us eat ourselves alive in a mirror.

EURYDICE. Expendable beasts.

CORTAENIA. Yes, yes, expendable beasts.

Pause.

Because all we ever do is argue and bleed, argue and bleed.

EURYDICE. What if I translated motions of the sundial for you? If I could get the mirrors to throb, the waters to run from the grain stores, and burn three delicate lakes within lanterns, I know you would fully see, without subsidy, the cusp of a star within water. As for me, I would double your palpable sonar and I know my arm would start to radiate again.

CORTAENIA. Such strange solutions. Look, I will never see the map of Vallejo's pre-exile or escape the blackened Ritalin cubes which always describe themselves in my throat.

EURYDICE. Then how do you know that you're not speaking to yourself?

CORTAENIA. What do you mean…

EURYDICE. Speaking to yourself. I can feel your eyes go dry behind the glasses.

>CORTAENIA *attempts to stand but falls back into her former sitting intensity.*

CORTAENIA. Now I'm a sum of gradations of pronounced elliptical parts.

>*Pause.*

Your arm smells like old urine.

EURYDICE. *Loudly.* It's the furnace.

CORTAENIA. *Yelling.* Turn it off!

>EURYDICE *makes no attempt to shut off the heater and continues her maniacal circling.*

EURYDICE. You're saying I make you miserable as if you could decipher glances over stadia.

CORTAENIA. Don't you know that the Sun can cast spells, that even the voodoo doctors waver.
EURYDICE. You threaten me. You imply that I'm taking risks by circling you in this manner. If I handed you a shoot of flowers from my grave, if I blessed them with spontaneous rapprochement, you would nevertheless find something evil in the way my verbal appearance was rendered.

>*Pause.*

I would lose salt from my person and would seem to burn in a naked kind of rust, hounded, and hounded again, oh how I know you can hound, Cortaenia.

CORTAENIA. I've only known you for forty-nine days.

EURYDICE. *Slightly mocking.* But, Cortaenia, it's a circumstantial flaw, a destinal chastisement, a revolt within oblivion.

> *Pause.*

Remember, in a past birth you told me that your mother was a Spanish courtesan during the rule of Vespasian and that you could take on three men during the grip of adolescence.

CORTAENIA. Your teeth are forced open.

EURYDICE. You told me this eight and half days ago. That you tumbled from a gladiator's pouch. That you literally milked pleasure from the wicked.

> CORTAENIA *stumbles from her chair and attempts to slap* EURYDICE, *who reacts with her one healthy arm, rudely pushing* CORTAENIA *back into her original sitting position.*

> *Mockingly.*

You can't even see from the distance from which you hear. And trying to attack me when you know this is what you said.

CORTAENIA. *Shaking.* There's a difference between poise and naturally defending the boundary of the Sun. And I will continue to defend the boundary of the Sun!

EURYDICE. You're confused like a sun between eclipse and sonar.

CORTAENIA. You leper! You slash your arm, you terrify your family, then claim the right to sympathy. You are a monger who'd like to ride and shoe me like a pony, dusk, after dusk, after dusk.

EURYDICE. Stop rhyming and burning up threads in a dungeon.

Pause.

Tell me, have you ever thought that your blindness was a paralytic series of vague announcements? Perhaps before you were born you were queen of the Archons and now your husk is overthrown into time.

CORTAENIA. Baseless!

EURYDICE. But you've responded. You know you were once invisible and held the charm of life and death over lions.

CORTAENIA. Rhetoric!

EURYDICE. *Emphatically.* Aren't you the Sun?

CORTAENIA. Every time you revolve there is a detrimental pain, a diabology, a devastation.

EURYDICE. If I move with anti-adroitness…

Hesitates.

it is because you scare me, watching you sit in that chair day after day, conniving, conniving, conniving.

EURYDICE *begins to slowly stop her circling motion and begins silently weeping, wiping her eyes with the sleeves of her gown. She never really ceases to move but at certain points in her circling movement is almost imperceptible.*

CORTAENIA. I can hear you panicking.

EURYDICE. *Moving again with more perceptible force.* If I die it is you who vicariously hemorrhages.

CORTAENIA. So you mean you want to occupy denial and dredge up the ghosts in between us.

EURYDICE. I never said such a thing.

CORTAENIA. But that's what you mean when you attempt to cut the blisters from my throat and leave me singing like a boiling sunbird in blood.

EURYDICE. Why should I accept what you say when I know it's ice, nothing but murderous ice?

    Pause.

You keep hacking and reattaching my body, just to wear me away, so that I fall into labored encampments.

CORTAENIA. Stop defending yourself so rudely.

EURYDICE. I'm not defending anything. You attack me…

CORTAENIA. All I hear are riddles and dust, riddles and dust…

EURYDICE. *Beginning to circle in a menacing manner.* If I'm erratic then you've created your horror. I arrived after you and have every right to convict my own position. Examining my soul is like parting a fluid, which no longer exists.

CORTAENIA. It's strange how you offer this posthumous challenge and I'm supposed to deny it so as to rationalize intentions towards you.

EURYDICE. Challenge…

CORTAENIA. Yes, challenge. Because I know you want me dead. I can feel the way you've been hovering around me over these latter three days. Look at it practically: you have the use of one arm practically emptied of blood, you have no knife with which to stab me. To strangle me, your force is too weak, then you become en-stormed by emotions, which converge into evil, then the rest of your energy turns into despair.

EURYDICE. *In a slightly trembling voice.* I never said I wanted to kill you or mention any evil against you. I need you to re-double your sonar so that my arm can live again.

ACT THREE

EURYDICE *erratically circles* CORTAENIA *with lessening resolve. The singing continues to sussurate from the shadows into the diffuse white light, until* CORTAENIA *begins to intone.*

CORTAENIA. You want to know how to summon up and break down the poisons. This is the way abstraction works. It is power conducted through sensation, like the blind touching of brass or feeling the way advance blizzards record.

EURYDICE. *Reflective.* When my blood would soak the cabinets and make finger stains on the cups, it was because I knew my arm had gone dead. And by making newer fresher injuries, I felt somehow that it would activate necrosis.

CORTAENIA. Even if I could forthrightly see, I would abstain from peering at your visual presence, I would refuse the way you've conducted your affairs, I would testify to the infinite against the electricity of your ethers.

EURYDICE. *Stilled, yet nervously standing at a right angle to the chair.* So you reject my revolutions, these inspired recriminations and exile. You'd love it if I was simple and you could crush me and creatively waver in the blood. It would allow you to summon up oracular philosophies, to burn within a ruse of dark stances. By igniting this embarkation you would be able to burden and reclaim your burden with sudden tenacity and panache, then each avalanche on the Sun would become a blessing of strange cerulean gifts, the core of your sodden fingers then able to compose in the manner of Malebranche a treatise on separation of being.

31

As EURYDICE *resumes the strength of her earlier circumambulation* CORTAENIA *seems to intensify her muscular state.*

CORTAENIA. You're doing nothing but drifting and blowing with your breath a bevy of blunted Thracian rapiers at me. A despicable proto-archery. And I say this, not because Cortaenia is blind, but because you attack my raw succession of address as it tends to plentify local space with direction.

EURYDICE. Then how many times will you blacken and divide my name? How many times will you brew the energies in my veins with sullen disadvantage?

CORTAENIA. I am not...

EURYDICE. *With anger.* You are brewing disadvantage, Cortaenia, taking care so as to flaunt the crosses in your teeming rectal church, being mistress at the encyclical pitch of malefic hosannas.

CORTAENIA. You ridicule because you feel I somehow stare through you. That I witness your genes in entangled combination. Because it is true, I have a second set of doubled solar eyes, only matched by doubled greenness and rainbows.

EURYDICE. Because of you, how can any fear exfoliate its density?

CORTAENIA. Yes, I am sand-blind, but my eyes suggest accoutrements implied by angelic penetralia. And the accoutrements are Asiatic and transmute their powers by means of malignant tiger skins.

EURYDICE. So how can I tell that you see me?

CORTAENIA. Because my inner anthems resonate. Because each impersonal optic has a shifting level of invisible greenness.

Pause.

Perhaps if I existed by lying prone for hundreds of hours you could dispute my example with overwhelming complaint. You could maniacally warp me with a summary of funereal happenstance, of colorless brine, of antipodean emotion. You could say that my sweltering was a postmortem tactical analysis, brought back from the lower Bardo as a supreme fundamental rigidity. As total eclipse imprisonment, aligned with a cold and intrinsic divisiveness. How could the Sun have potential, how could it produce antelopes or rye or aggressive moray behavior?

EURYDICE. Being parallel to your existence, do you honestly think that I am looking for social lesions or an indifferent planetary victory?

Pause.

Do you honestly feel that I have extracted surcease from the hallucinatory eyes of the catacombs? That I stagger for water every two thousand daybreaks, mineral and listless, with a wild potassium synopsis?

CORTAENIA. So should I take this as blundering? As debasement under panic? Or should I gather asteroids at your poles and proclaim a December conflagration according to the dictates engendered at the peak of Olympus Mons?

EURYDICE. Now your mockery tends to sophisticate itself, to in-grow its larder with wrangling.

CORTAENIA. No, you're only deadly with envy.

33

EURYDICE. Because of your claims to see greenness, how could I wish to kill—your flames, your fraudulent testament, divided helical neurosis?

CORTAENIA. But the storm exists, Eurydice. The State has claimed us as exfoliate negativities, much the equal of coelacanths. As subspecies of the living.

   Pause.

Even you set fire to your blood and leave ambiguous offspring to rot in the hovels of Tunisia.

EURYDICE. I could think in Tunisia and strengthen my own force from a healthy lunation so every month that I was pregnant I would transmute subliminal nightmares within the coruscating powers of my stomach.

CORTAENIA. Would you destroy a sullen offspring, would you take away its strength before fruition?

EURYDICE. How could I be so blatant, Cortaenia? How could I have them stifled in a psychic scorpion forest, their integument turned to droplets, entered partway in a mirror, that is everyday somehow exploded?

CORTAENIA. By the time my blindness set in my uncles took lots as to how much raping my appetite could take. They even claimed that the bed slats were red from the blood each intercourse engendered. I was threatened with disclosure, even if a child poured forth from their contradictive celebrations.

EURYDICE. You're barren then.

CORTAENIA. Whoever I said was barren and incapable of producing babies' milk.

EURYDICE. You imply impermanent glandular deficits, you imply stalking and harassment. By the time I was born they implanted denial in my system and brutally enacted self-hatred. And I began to slash myself and cause worry and burn my own blood in a personally erected canister. Anything to feel pain, anything to re-create sensation.

CORTAENIA. We are doomed and tragically ballistic from birth. Your genes have brought you to this wavering, to this pre-clinical era of punctured sundials and herons.

EURYDICE. But what do you know about my height, its brush against limbo, its negative ebullience?

CORTAENIA. So how was I born?

EURYDICE. It was a hot winter day within the redolent confines of Cairo. Your parents were staggering in Tunisian, with your father being Iraqi and Jewish. You were born in Magdalena and scorched by specific twists in morality. And this beyond any suicidal canister of blood.

CORTAENIA. I can see as well and I dispute your libidinous pointing.

EURYDICE. *Intensely.* Stop it, Cortaenia, stop backing away from the vacuum!

　　Pause.

Your curse has been sculpted to singe and re-singe my lesions.

CORTAENIA. You're stymied, Eurydice.

EURYDICE. You've ransacked make-believe authority to take out hate on the void, in order to lash out, to ruin, to dissipate your anti-conception.

CORTAENIA. *Anxiously.* What do you mean I can't conceive?

EURYDICE. Your helium counts are low, your hydrogen base has been stricken.

CORTAENIA. No, you speak in terms of a stricken anti-ideal, a mythic blood-loss gone badly.

EURYDICE. Perhaps you suggest I switch faces with a hapless Minoan charioteer, eerily prior to the vomiting of Therea.

CORTAENIA. Am I implying apocalypse or mingling a verbal finery with sudden exuviations? I'm simply feeling the traces within your injured psychic locale, within its stricken history of maiming.

EURYDICE. *Angered.* What's the purpose of your probing? To eat away at my innards, to take away my habitat and blind it?
CORTAENIA. Now you speak as if I had girdled you in proverbial bondage.

EURYDICE. Go back to Magdalena, go back to your swill and poisoned griffin meat.

CORTAENIA. Don't you see? That's why they want to kill us and record our conversations, like old Madame Ceasescu when she monitored her soldiers' lovemaking bouts.

EURYDICE. You mean the flesh and blood mirror.

CORTAENIA. Yes, the flesh and blood mirror.

Pause.

Things go on in these places that we, as their crippled enemies, can no longer combat with massive hernial attacks or juxtaposition of chemicals in the brain. If we complain about the smells...

EURYDICE. I know, Cortaenia. I shake the roaches from my dressing gown and sadistically crush them as they scurry through the darkness in fever. And this is more my daily life than ever.

CORTAENIA. I dreamed two days ago that with your one sound arm you pulled me over a barricade and there I witness Alpacas, and Caimans, and Cocoa, and Mahogany.

EURYDICE. Was it like pre-birth or illusive selenium fogs?

CORTAENIA. No, we escaped and became obscurely united with old Sumerian beggar gods and gained by sudden beauty a pure and maniacal ruthlessness.

EURYDICE. But even in this dream you describe you contain, you torment the contents with an inverse arrangement. I think of errors, of broodings, of ignited and culpable spite.

CORTAENIA. It is war, Eurydice, war. Why? Because we are of singular curiosity. We suggest a zone of infernal resplendence, of watchworks by which sphinxes salivate, by which exquisite paradox is enhanced.

Pause.

It makes them violent and somehow wary of our powers.

Pause.

First, we were invaded with incarceration, then they charge us with mumbling in allostoephas, in tides burning against their solemn lingual fronts. Our allegiance to ruse as psychic depletion.

EURYDICE. Is this our symbolic dishonor, our covenant with the millstone?

She pauses and begins shaking.

No, this can't be, this can't have priority in existence. In thirty years I'll continue within the bounds of active voltage and only have as my optical ground the shattered windows of a vermin castle.

CORTAENIA. Perhaps through de-active explosion they will attempt to condemn our rich brown skin into experimental memory. To erase our kinetic parallels, our titanic sabbaticals.

EURYDICE. My feelings tell me that the ministerial houses will soon vanish. Europe will soon take the form of a cloudy Nubian acreage. That the Christos will soon flee into a maze of ghostly windmill houses and we'll sing like fanatic Galapagos hawks in ill-begotten coloratura.

CORTAENIA. You mean all the English surnames will fall, all their old plutonic gifts will vanish.

EURYDICE. Their national histories will begin to burn as bloody amorphic refuse, as mazes caught up in Teutonic calendars of mayhem.

CORTAENIA. And we, post-atomic salamander lions.

EURYDICE. For us, as salamander lions, the northern zones will be useless, the peoples will have lost their thread of measured conquering identity.

CORTAENIA. I've felt this intrinsic fire in my spores, this basic rapture of uranian suspension, as though all my spores were fire, the fire of my cellular integument of spores.

EURYDICE. I feel the absence of relapse, of journeys back to caesium, of falsely riddled turpitude.

CORTAENIA. Therefore we take from brokenness a message or a hawk, across scattered lamps and trees. It is the necessary ritual. Then you exist with anodyne eyes, seeing farther than the optical doctors call tell you, the latter being part of the species malforming into disappearance.

   Pause.

Even in my darkest moments I've always urged on the power of the catacombs and the beatific stench of its strange Elysium cunning.

EURYDICE. The Elysium, Cortaenia, the Elysium!

CORTAENIA. Did I hear you say the void will abstain itself from fragments and bring on a lagoon of massive estrogen hauling, of astral lagoons and insight?

EURYDICE. A massive scale above the imbibing of powder, shall we say?

CORTAENIA. Powder in the ways of sluicing the flesh, with currents at an angle, where types of blood exchange in a movement of arrows. Both my arms would hang inside land and I'd find myself in a tumultuous new sea, under anti-quotidian branches.

EURYDICE. You think like a black and curly ibis, knowing the true powers of failure, gnomic, crystalline, without color.

Pause.

Quintessential, like consciousness, as in a Hittite plague or a samurai's emotion.

Pause.

So if we begin to bleed, can that save us, can that deliver us from co-dependence with God? Can we then possess the power to strike our own arms with grace and hurdle the coming utopian carnage amidst the utter roaring of mimes?

CORTAENIA. Look, Eurydice, our blades have stuck in these theories of salvos, so that I am committed to a second waking, to a crisis, where the body is thrown aside, to re-arise in disputation.

EURYDICE. To strip the body of its respirating ornaments.

CORTAENIA. That is partial, but your body must rise above the eclipse sullage and take on the fever within the fate of a bodiless vortex, completely foreign to the duplicitous power of history, so as to transform our beacons, blending roots with darkened oneiric aftermaths.

> CORTAENIA *takes on a more intense solemnity.*

Then the cells must be lightened and the void traversed within them, so that they aviate above the ignited branch of gravity.

EURYDICE. So if I sought to levitate my body I would become its simultaneous witness, its conduction through metaphysical fiber,

40

devoid of frontality or theatrics.

Pause.

A magic ink, a tensely permeable cholera.

CORTAENIA. I'm seeking advice on my blindness, on the drawn strips of color, which elude me or shift in the haze, like letters or bunting or the vicious illusives of ambiguous movement.

EURYDICE. I would please you immensely if I became the prototype of Vesta or Ceres or a careening fragment without any anchoring fire.

CORTAENIA. I am allowing you opening to leap to new imaginal suns, to new and indifferent revolving tornadoes.

EURYDICE. What do you mean? A new debility, another abstract roundness?

CORTAENIA. I believe you want to see my blood and perceive its action as a river across the Sun.

EURYDICE. I'm not a vampire, Cortaenia!

CORTAENIA. *Becoming frantic.* Why do you deny it? Why do you deny the opposite, that you're trapped, that I've informed your rationales by nefarious justification?

EURYDICE. You only justify aggression and I'm tired of your oily penchant for digging up a grave worms!

CORTAENIA. I can only say that your anchors are dimming, Eurydice, that your poles are falling inward against the stars.

EURYDICE. *Mockingly.* Then you imply the hidden jonquil urns in your eyes.

Pause.

I suppose you heinously rejoice every time you explode a sovereign planetary discourse, every time that fetid corona destroys a type of weather within a world.

CORTAENIA. You're jaundiced because I still absorb the general grace of the heavens with the angle of my deep absorption winds, with the power of my paradoxical coronas.

EURYDICE. No, you want to throw me off balance, to implant treason in my spine, so that I'll shatter, so that you can live within a bleak but momentary quadrennial!

She suddenly grabs CORTAENIA *by the throat.*
Now, if I can crack the slaver in your skull wide open...

CORTAENIA *breaks free of her enfeebled grip and awkwardly stands up and grabs the living arm of* EURYDICE *and bites the heel of her hand, drawing blood.* EURYDICE *screams.* CORTAENIA *then staggers about, trying to locate her cane and her chair. As she continues to stumble, she wildly peers in all directions, maliciously screaming at* EURYDICE.

CORTAENIA. Now your waters fragment and bleed and the stars deny you rhythm and your ethers bring spells and deliriums and entangle your threats in the dice of meridians...

Her voice fades. EURYDICE *then bends on one knee and buries her face in her one living palm as the lights go dim with a strange ringing of bells.*

ZOMAYA AND THE MYRMIDONS

A Play in Three Acts

Characters:
ZOMAYA, Matriarch, mid 40's, an uncanny mixture of youthful vigor and authoritative demeanor.

ORACULOS, Oldest brother, 39, lean, nervous, wary, defensive.

ESTEBAN, Nearly the same build as Oraculos. Slightly shorter in stature, drunken, subservient, sporadically violent, almost always partially covered in shadow. He is the middle brother, 27.

JESUS, Darkest in coloration. A strange unhappiness in his aggression. Shortest in stature, 25

Place:
New Mexico. Home of a reclusive aristocratic Mexican family.

Time:
Present day.

ACT ONE

A darkish sitting room. A small flowered couch representative of bygone decades, angled downstage left, so that the sitting position of each character is always 3/4 facing the audience. Across from the couch a pine colored coffee table, atop which set books, which include a book on pharmacology, and a glossary on magic. There is a single pine colored chair facing the couch always partially shadowed. ORACULOS sitting tensed at the edge of the couch pulls from the coffee table the glossary on magic and begins nervously thumbing through it. ZOMAYA then enters from a door stage left, attired in a black scarf and a longish black dress. She is a bit unnerved, but composed.

ORACULOS. What did she say? *Anxiously looking up at* ZOMAYA. Did the nuns treat you strangely?

ZOMAYA. *In a stern, almost mocking tone.* What do you mean, strangely.

ORACULOS. You know I can't visit. If I show my face suspicions will start boiling.

ZOMAYA. *Definitively.* That's why I can't tell you everything because I know you'll panic, you'll anul all our gifts of protection.

ORACULOS. *Still sitting, intently glaring at* ZOMAYA. It's your way of trying to keep power, of keeping me stung by obliqueness.

ZOMAYA. *Raising her voice slightly.* I tell you what's of value, isn't that enough. She bathes, she eats twice a day, and she wanders around in her mind.

ORACULOS. *Partially angered.* It's not enough Zomaya, not now, things have gone too far.

Pause.

ZOMAYA. *Smoldering.* She looks the same, but she just chatters.

ORACULOS. You know her tongue is a wick, and she'll consume us; she'll burn us until we're empty.

ZOMAYA. *Pulling off her scarf, sitting down on the chair at the table.* Why are you so worried about consumption. You're already famished. You don't have a person. You're skeletal Oraculos, that's the only way I can put it.

ORACULOS. No, you avoid what I'm saying. You know when you speak to her, that you drain the blood from your tongue and then attempt to implode my expectations with this fatigue.

Pause.

With recrimination. Your own brother, your own brother!

ZOMAYA. Stop it! *Leaning forward on her elbows.* Haven't you always been drained. Your ethos is regret subtracted from regret.

ORACULOS. *Head raised.* Mock me then, bleed me, implant my skull with leeches!

Pause.

Lowering his intensity. You remember, I only asked you what she said, how she injected her anger into her feelings.

ZOMAYA. I give her tapes, that's all she asks for, tapes.

ORACULOS. Does she mention…

ZOMAYA. She doesn't mention your name. Do I think she's forgotten you, no? But she never mentions your name.

ORACULOS. *Momentary relief. Leans back somewhat on the couch and breathes deeply.* But what about the tapes?

ZOMAYA. The nuns say that she talks to herself nightly, they say she mumbles syllables to herself.

ORACULOS. She's been there over seven months and you've always evaded even this paltry description. You've emitted to me vagaries, about the curtains, about the strands of light, the iguana colored candles, which litter her room.

ZOMAYA. You're splintered Oraculos If it wasn't for me all three of you would be instantly condemned; the state would inject your veins with cyanide.

ORACULOS. *In a heightened voice.* Then you admit you're evil; that you're a foundry of pure venom.

ZOMAYA. *Her back arched between standing and sitting.* You accuse me like this, you who has had my body the most often, who has entered my body like a hellish flambeau.

ORACULOS bows his head, un-tenses his shoulders. Then ESTEBAN appears looming in partial shadows stage right with what one would call an imperceptible gloating.

Pause.

Esteban, bring Jesus to me. ESTEBAN *lingers.* Now!

ESTEBAN. He's sleeping.

ZOMAYA. Then wake him!

ESTEBAN then disappears stage right and quickly reappears as ZOMAYA having left her chair paces back and forth in front of ORACULOS without stopping. A disheveled JESUS then emerges from the shadows stage right, his starched white shirt wrinkled, half tucked in his pants, rubbing his eyes, trying to cast off sleep, yet marked by a trace of defiance. He and ESTEBAN stand behind the couch at angles to one another. ZOMAYA stops pacing and directly faces the three of them.

ZOMAYA. *Authoritatively.* All of you, all of you, trapped inside my blood. If I breathe a certain way all of your lungs react in kind. If I emit curses in my sleep you all stay maimed for days on end. Since Oraculos touched me first he has prime responsibility.

Manically pointing to ESTEBAN and JESUS.

You are my tragically sheltered bulls.

She then begins intensely pacing back and forth within a compacted distance.

Exasperated. How can I continue this way with the three of you always supping at my flesh?

JESUS. So you've tasted our sperm, but what other rights do you have over us other than a wicked spider's foundation.

ZOMAYA. I've never trusted you, Jesus…

JESUS. It's the Olmec in me. It's my heated spinal delirium.

ESTEBAN. He's right Zomaya. You've eaten a fraction of inclement

47

wood and all you leave are bloody lunar traces.

  He pauses, and then begins slowly walking towards ZOMAYA *partially covered by shadow. His speech slightly slurred.*

It's all those old hereditary stains. It's the poisoned snake inside your womb.

ZOMAYA. You smell like rum.

  ESTEBAN inches slowly forward, his outstretched right arm aggressively pointing his rum cup towards her face; ORACULOS quickly standing glances sidelong at ESTEBAN.

ORACULOS. *Forcefully.* Stop it, Esteban!

ESTEBAN. *His speech slurred.* What do you mean stop? She gives me money and I drink; and this drink kills all the bickering in me.

JESUS. *His voice slightly strained.* What do you know about Zomaya? How can you tell him anything? *Pointing at* ORACULOS.

  Moving parallel to ESTEBAN.

We're brothers.

ZOMAYA. *Still standing, practically shouting.* Then why don't you leave, why don't you test yourselves in life! Move wood, carry water in the sun!

  JESUS seethes; ORACULOS looks at her warily.

Your father left me as sole arbiter of the profits from his secretive liquor hives; and what I've done is nothing more than give and give and give.

JESUS. *Mockingly.* So you're that great Duchess, the angelic benefactress, the eagle who dives from a soothsayer's cage and gives bread.

ZOMAYA. *Glaring at* ESTEBAN. What did that black frock cost you?

> *She walks into the partial shadow and begins feeling the material, and then as quickly walks back to her former standing position next to the pine chair.*

> *Silence.*

> *Erupts.* You waste, you do nothing but waste!

ESTEBAN. And what do you do? Scheme with Oraculos, study henbane texts, so that you can practice protracted poisoning leaving you both with the spoils.

ZOMAYA. Only a swine would utter...

ESTEBAN. No, you're the swine Zomaya.

> *A look of hatred then passes back and forth between* ORACULOS *and* JESUS.

ZOMAYA. Do you realize that they separately disowned us just days before they died too weak to change the papers concerning the money that we live on. Just two weeks, the one, then the other. And did any of you weep? Did any of you feel compelled to join them in the grave?

JESUS. *Angrily.* And why did they disown us? *Staring intently at* ZOMAYA. Because you couldn't keep your hands off Oraculos. You couldn't be the respectful older sister, withdrawn, stunning, oblique.

ESTEBAN. I know Oraculos. He's nothing but an impoverished dandy. And you, Miss Queen Viper.

ORACULOS. *To* ESTABAN. You're full of rum and hives!

JESUS. No, you're the fool Oraculos, and now worried about what Rosanna will say.

ORACULOS *stares at* JESUS *silently, then sits back down on the couch and buries his head in his hands.*

Pause.

We have no reputation. Any respect we garner has lesions. No one claims us as offsprings. Surname as spawned in Cimmeria. Sometimes I play with using the English surname Donovan, or strangely thinking that someone will describe my apparition as Jesus Bell.

ESTEBAN. *Spitting.* Surname as mud.

ZOMAYA. *A sinister smirch on her face.* Realize that all your cells have been wedded to catastrophe. *She then turns to* ORACULUOS. Tell them about your richness of aspiration. Tell them about the astronomy you claim to study.

ORACULOS. *In a slightly broken voice raising his head.* The laws of weather in Venus, the telepathic explosions on Mars. *Nervously.* I mean the prime factor of impact.

ZOMAYA. Let me ask you this Oraculos; what about mountain building, what about the different forms of rational volcanoes?

JESUS. *A general viciousness in his voice.* You're prompting Zomaya.

ORACULOS. *Holding his head slightly higher, a nascent sincerity in his voice.* No, I want to speak of a different gage of blood, of a species capable of thriving on alien absolutes, on scattering alphabets to the outer asteroids.

ESTEBAN. But what good does that do you if Zomaya has shaken your basic mental traces.

Pause.

You are weakened by petty optical crimes, by solutions, which show no exhibit.

ORACULOS. *Standing again. Confronting* ESTEBAN. How do you know that the galaxies we see have always occupied elective position? How do you know if the cells from your body evolved from some reclusive brown dwarf?

Pause

See, you waver; you must know that immensity precedes concentration, that the concentration that we call Esteban has no ultimate concentration in perceptible reality. No impact Esteban, no impact. In this one temperature that we know as present time, perhaps hydrogen...

ESTEBAN. *Less slurred, slightly mocking.* Perhaps I'm broken ambrosia, perhaps I stutter from need.

Pause.

You have her more than Jesus and I combined, that is why life is more circular for you.

JESUS. *Sinisterly laughs, glaring at* ORACULOS. Now you can

51

imbibe auroras from her belly, taste the clammy powder on her breath. It's like putting a cup of heroin in my veins. I float, I hover in eclectic pleasure.

ZOMAYA. So Jesus, are you claiming to improve existence? Are you claiming the powers of hereditary blackmail?

Pause.

All you do is sleep and condemn that which wakes. *Accusatory.* Admit it Jesus, it's the heroin, it's always the heroin. You slip its power into your veins, and you mesmerize viewing a nightless moment on Ceres, or watch yourself in a cloudy kayak tournament, or feel that you figure the mathematics in a stripped botanical lean-to.

JESUS. You're just propping him up because of Rosanna.

Pause.

Moves sluggishly from the shadows to confront ZOMAYA face to face.

You created her, now you put her away in that old despicable nunnery.

ZOMAYA *slaps him, and* ORACULOS *immediately restrains him;* ESTEBAN *imbibes a cup of rum and menacingly spits it out on the floor.*

ESTEBAN. So if I kill you, Oraculos, all the money is ruined. Zomaya will disappear and change identity. You know it's true.

ORACULOS *then hurls* JESUS *into the darkness behind the couch tensing as though* ESTEBAN *were ready to attack him.*

ZOMAYA. *Screaming at all three of them.* Look at me! If I gave you all a list of assets you'd aggravate me by false debate on the spacing of the items. To me, you're nothing but negligible progeny. Castoffs. Your lungs blurred, diseases creeping around your eyes!

Pause.

None of you can forget that I'm responsible for your eating.

JESUS. *Sitting on his knees, leaning against the back of the couch.* You're responsible for nothing, absolutely nothing.

ZOMAYA. Then how do you eat, who pays for your habit?

ESTEBAN. You always create confusion, Zomaya. You like to scatter us, and then gather us like spoiled amoebas.

ORACULOS *and* ESTEBAN *now hurriedly glancing back and forth at each other, then the two of them starting at* ZOMAYA.

ZOMAYA. *Cynically.* Get drunk Esteban. *She rushes back to the coffee table and opens her purse, and turns back towards* ESTEBAN *and aggressively tosses several hundred-dollar bills in the direction of* ESTEBAN *and* JESUS. Jesus, is that enough tot finish cooking your circulation?

ESTEBAN *throws his rum cup at* ZOMAYA, *then proceeds with* JESUS *to slowly pick up the money as if trying to elicit some further form of confrontation.* ORACULOS *imperceptibly inches towards* ZOMAYA *like heat drawn towards heat, as* ESTEBAN *and* JESUS *jealously glower at them while gathering the money. The room darkens as the curtain slowly falls.*

ACT TWO

ESTEBAN *and* JESUS *retreat out of view stage right like animals into their lair. The couch and coffee table dimly lit as in the first act. The shadows from which* ESTEBAN *and* JESUS *have retreated still persist. Having parted from a lascivious embrace,* ORACULOS *returns to the couch,* ZOMAYA *having returned to the chair facing* ORACULOS; *her longish dress practically pulled up to her thighs.*

ZOMAYA. *In a rapt, sensitive tone.* I can't go on with them. *Looking intensely at* ORACULOS.

 Pause.

Do something.

ORACULOS. What do you want me to do? Kill them? Then the bodies would turn up, and all our attempts at peace would be shattered. Is this what you want, Zomaya? Isn't it bad enough?

ZOMAYA. Then why do I keep you if you can't do the essential things I ask for.

ORACULOS. *Looking intently at* ZOMAYA. Why at this point lie. Why fool yourself. I couldn't separate myself from your heat.

 Slowly dropping his head. Getting up from the chair. ZOMAYA *goes to the couch and draws close to* ORACULOS *grabbing his hands, holding them tightly.*

ZOMAYA. But you're weak, Oraculos, blaming the dead for keeping us trapped. You refer to our parentage like worn carpet or old data.

 Pause.

They created us. *Slowly letting go his hands.*

ORACULOS. But just like an alligator caresses eggs; they didn't want us.

He sighs.

How could they implant us with this burden and just disown us near the time of death. I'm certain Martha spread rumors about Rosanna when you were pregnant. And like you they believed in the hellish though they day to day confessed. At times I wanted to make Rosanna unreal. But when Martha…

ZOMAYA. *Almost whimpering.* They left us money.

ORACULOS. But I'm bereft, I can't work, I can't liquidate my ancient ptomaine certificates.

> *Pause.*

Martha is all that she's good for. And since he disowned us at the border of the void, I'll refer to my father as Senor Oblivious. I just remember him as being an old albino leopard. So I only feel alive when I touch you.

ZOMAYA. You're weak, Oraculos, just like Esteban and Jesus. You should have left me by now. Our child is almost grown and what she says may purge any resistance that we carry.

ORACULOS *begins trembling with anger and disgust.*

ORACULOS. So what about the tapes that you gave her?

ZOMAYA. You carry this ridiculous burden. I told you, she doesn't say anything, the incest made her blind.

ORACULOS. But what does she say on the tapes?

ZOMAYA. *Angrily.* You've never seen her as she is.

ORACULOS. She's a savant, she utters in nervous lightning rapier.

> *Nervously pauses.*

You've unhinged her scribblings on suicide. You didn't know that but I do. Instead of the tapes why didn't you just give her something to hold or to smell? I tell you she's holding vapor against us. Every time I lie with you I feel the dissonance she causes.

ZOMAYA. *Drawing further away.* She's your daughter too.

> *Pause.*

The nuns think you're a runaway to Venezuela; that you were victim of a shipwreck, and that you wander across Caracas as one who simply vanished.

ORACULOS. It's implausible Zomaya. How can they believe that not a single trace is left.

ZOMAYA. I say it with such sincerity that it's plausible. That you were distraught at the death of our parents and simply vanished in to the world. I've told them that I've made searches for you in Caracas, that I've mingled with authorities, that the possibility exists that you've been absorbed into the continent, that quite possible you're dead.

ORACULOS. *Somewhat anxious.* What about the others? What about Esteban and Jesus?

ZOMAYA. They were never registered with numbers. They were born here at home, the midwife knew no English, and Jose and Martha hid them away as people, just as I'm hiding you now, Oraculos.

ORACULOS. But she knows me; I've had her repeatedly, she...

ZOMAYA. *Again drawing closer to* ORACULOS. She knows you only by the penetration of your member. Oraculos, she just chatters, she just simply chatters.

ORACULOS. No, you're hiding something from me; it's like a disrupted sigil. I see a dismembered reptile, green, crawling in different directions.

ZOMAYA. *Pulling away again.* You'd rather see her dead than speak. You remind me of a bear with its teeth broken down to the nectar.

ORACULOS. *Shifting uncomfortably.* So what do you tell Esteban and Jesus when they suck you, when they play with your nipples, when you slip powder in my coffee? *More heatedly.* What do you tell them?

ZOMAYA *pulls further away, avoiding his glance.*

ZOMAYA. I told you she's doing fine. I pay the nuns every Thursday and I go. When I first brought her in, I told them the father was missing, and the burden of her blindness too strong for me to care for. It's a very oblique maturation, Oraculos, but they respect me. *Her voice slightly breaks.* It's the first time I've had respect and so I just sit with Rosanna, we just sit and think. We know that we're telepathically entangled.

ORACULOS. *Without warning, he suddenly grabs her by the throat.* You know something Zomaya, you want me blackmailed, and you keep me weakened simply by the act of pure evil.

ZOMAYA. *Gasping.* You're hurting me.

He let's her go, and she begins shaking her head to somehow absolve herself of the pain. ORACULOS *then gets up and circles the couch and stops standing in front of her.*

ORACULOS. You've made it so that I can't even conjure a sacrifice, or paint a doll's face with semen.

    Putting his hands momentarily to his face.

And you won't stop it. You hate to see me at peace. You hate to hear me conjure out loud my thoughts about the heavens.

    Pause.

Almost frantic. Make Esteban and Jesus leave. You have powers, use them!

ZOMAYA. *Regaining some of her strength.* They're probably asleep. Be a man, go kill them. *She gets up and goes back stage left into the darkness and quickly returns with* ORACULOS *turned and staring at her.* Here is a bag of the purest heroin I could get. The needles are clean, I'll even cook it for you.

ORACULOS *stunned.*

ORACULOS. Just kill them?

ZOMAYA. Yes, just kill them, just inject them with doses, and if they trace it back to you, just sleep off the blood in a cell.

ORACULOS. So you want to just sacrifice me. Contaminate me with murder and leave yourself free of any fixation.

He starts aimlessly wandering back and forth across the stage, then falls backward onto the couch exhausted.

ZOMAYA. You see, I can't kill because I'm the responsible party. If the blame rests with me, none of us exists. You've always been more than my brother. But I can't go on giving you money unless you inject them.

ORACULOS. *Wearily.* You just want to exhaust us. Just like a witch you drain venom from a rock, and envision our forms in the venom, and then let us burn in a river of nothingness.

ZOMAYA. *Standing over* ORACULOS. See, you do this to yourself. You enkindle a hatchery of omegas in your mind and it exhausts you. Tell yourself this. Nothing of what I think is true. Keep saying it to yourself, nothing of what I think is true, then a magical kind of liberty will flow into your actions.

She begins pacing in front of ORACULOS.

As for now, I want you to beat back the hair snakes, and empty the doubt from your system. *Pointing to her head.* It's all in your mind. Do you know that all land and power is purchased by homicide. Then one's thought becomes strategic, and one then knows that loss is gain, and gain turns into nothing more than greater gain. There's ways of icing corpses until one burns them. I'll start making arrangements after you've done it.

ZOMAYA *then hands the two needles and the heroin to a completely numbed* ORACULOS, *and then returns to her chair staring at him intensely.*

A complete darkening of the stage as curtain falls.

59

ACT THREE

As before, ORACULOS *sits numbed;* ZOMAYA *gets up from her chair as if she were about to lasciviously arouse him to actions, when* ESTEBAN *enters groggily with a cup in his hand.*

ESTEBAN. Did you smother him?

ZOMAYA. You sot!

ESTEBAN. *His speech slurred.* You tricked him into thinking he could cast spells.

ZOMAYA. So you're telling me I can poison a fig tree with my glance, or invisibly trample a moral flag?

ESTEBAN. *Stumbling to the edge of the shadow.* Just give me money, Zomaya.

      ORACULOS *having cast the needles and the heroin from his hands, passively watches the confrontation.*

ZOMAYA. *Intensely.* I just gave you money. You can't remember if you live, or if death has approached you lately. But you won't leave. I open the darkness of your cave, the Sun falls in your eyes, and all you do is haunt me!

ESTEBEN. You need my embraces Zomaya. *Raising his cup.* To the concubine of the court of Persia!

ZOMAYA. If Rosanna wasn't living I'd take whatever life you've claimed by means of the sorcery of dogs.

ESTEBAN. All you do is pontificate, Zomaya. You remind me of those old common concubines who used to flood the street after a bout of bloodletting in Rome.

ZOMAYA. All I have to do is wait and you'll choke on your own mockery.

ESTEBAN. You smothered him.

ZOMAYA. How could I? I've been in this room since I returned from seeing Rosanna.

Pause.

He's just exhausted. He shoots a spoon of heroin a day.

ESTEBAN. No, you smothered him.

ZOMAYA. Stop accusing me and go and arouse him. I need everyone awake.

As ESTEBAN *begins to stagger back into the dark,* ORACULOS *begins sitting upright visibly fraught by tension.* ESTEBAN *staggers back into view alone drunkenly weeping.*

ESTEBAN. *Frightened.* I tried to wake him, I tried to rouse him with the needle, but he won't move, he just won't move.

ZOMAYA. He's your brother; just go back and revive him!

Pause.

Oraculos, go with him. Make sure he doesn't lie to me.

ORACULOS, *unable to move, turns his head away from* ZOMAYA *as though overcome by a bitter irritant;* ESTEBAN *then staggers back into the sitting room with a dazed look on his face.*

ESTEBAN. I can't revive him. *His voice cracking.* I keep shaking him and shaking him and he just won't move.

ZOMAYA. *Demonstratively.* Oraculos, help Esteban drag him in.

ORACULOS *moving very slowly getting up from the couch, his faced etched with inconceivable regret.*

Screaming into the darkness. I need his body in this room!

As ESTEBAN *and* ORACULOS *drag in the comatose* JESUS, ESTEBAN *looks up angrily at* ZOMAYA.

ESTEBAN. What do you want to do? Rape a man in a coma!

ZOMAYA. *Almost vociferous.* He's not in a coma. I know he's not in a coma. Just prop him against the couch and I'll feed him a special ice that I've made.

ZOMAYA *retreats stage left and returns with a smoldering cup of ice and begins to bathe the face and chest of* JESUS *with vigor;* ESTEBAN, *growing more and more sure, staggers back into the sleeping room without the notice of* ORACULOS *or* ZOMAYA. *One hears glass breaking as* ESTEBAN *emerges from the dark with a broken rum bottle jabbing at the air.*

ESTEBAN. Pretend that I am a surgeon from a country of acid, and you the Queen Zomaya, and the surgeon will carve the Queen.

ZOMAYA *standing up, moving backwards from the corpse of* JESUS, *instantly unsettled.*

ZOMAYA. Do something Oraculos! Do something! He's gone too far to live!

ORACULOS. *A dead quiet in his voice.* Drop the bottle, Esteban, just drop the bottle.

The tension concretizes as ESTEBAN *glowers at the both of them. No one moves.* ORACULOS *sweating profusely, suddenly flinches, and as he flinches,* ESTEBAN *hurls the bottle, barely missing* ZOMAYA'S *face.* ESTEBAN *then drops to one knee blankly staring at the floor. No one moves for some seconds. But one can feel* ZOMAYA *begin to regather composure.*

ZOMAYA. Oraculos, get me more ice. *Louder.* More ice.

ORACULOS *disappears into dark stage left and returns with a bowl, which again smolders with cold.* ESTEBAN *remains motionless.* ZOMAYA *resumes vigorously massaging the chest of* JESUS *with ice.*

ZOMAYA. *Pointing to* ORACULOS. Lay the body flat. I need to revive him. Go get the fish oil.

ORACULOS *again goes in to the dark stage right and returns with a bottle oil* ZOMAYA *then raises up the head of* JESUS *and attempts to force the oil down his gullet. Then without warning,* ORACULOS *suddenly kicks* ESTEBAN *several times so that he lays face first on the floor.* ORACULOS *then drags the corpse and again props it against the couch, as* ZOMAYA *stands drawing invisible diagrams in the air with her right index finger.*

ZOMAYA. Bring him back to life, Oraculos, you know forms from the engravings at Nineveh.

ORACULOS. There's a runnage of blood from his mouth.

ZOMAYA. Chant Oraculos, chant. We only ask for a number of morsels from the demons. Lightning or crab's flesh.

ORACULOS. He's ashen, Zomaya.

ZOMAYA. Then chant.

ESTEBAN *slowly staggering to his feet. Looking across at* ZOMAYA. This is how love has brought you power. You can lift my dead brother's head, but see how much you've failed.

Visibly shaken, ZOMAYA *begins wildly barking commands.*
ZOMAYA. Bring me more iodine and oil. Bring me a lantern, Oraculos. The flame will return intensity to his muscles.

She begins violently circling the corpse while continuing to rave.

Give him crushed gruel to drink. Flush a new gramme of simooms through his body. Reinvigorate his chakric ocean with new Egyptian mantras.

ORACULOS. *Bitterly.* You never recognized him, Zomaya. You knew he was wild and you gave him the powder to tame him, to make him strenuously gracious. But you never solved him. He was nothing but a beast to you and you've forced him to die.

ZOMAYA. *Attempting to brace herself.* Even now you're still jealous even though he's dead. It's because of the powerful welts he used to leave between my thighs. There's nothing you can do to match him, even if I continued to scream and tore at your eyes.

ESTEBAN. *Incoherent.* What about the powder inside my powers? What about the alligator fragments? What about the vulture's pots which continue to boil?

ZOMAYA. *Hurriedly.* Oraculos, I'll make the arrangements to have the body sealed in ice, and shipped to Mexico, and ignited in southern Durango. I'll tell the nuns to tell Rosanna that I hurt myself walking, and by going to Durango, I can create official delay through travel. I can create a paradigm of absence, then I can subtract the rot, drain the confusion.

ORACULOS. *Quietly chants.* Palas Aron Azinomas, Palas Aron Azinomas, Palas Aron Azinomas...

As ZOMAYA *fitfully falls on the corpse,* ESTEBAN *surreptitiously crawls, placing himself parallel to the bodies, weakly clawing at* ZOMAYA'S *twitching buttocks.*

INSIDE THE EARTHQUAKE PALACE

A Play in Three Acts

Characters:
GIOTTO. Afro-Italian from New York. Photographic aspirant.

RAPHAEL LOCATO. Prominent figure in the world of photography.
From Guyana, mid- 50's.

Place:
The Iguana Café in Plymouth, the capitol of Monserrat.

Time:
Pro to Monserrat's volcanic eruption. Late 20th Century.

ACT ONE

Rumbling noises, sight shaking of table and two chairs. GIOTTO *and* LOCATO *are sitting across from one another, intently conversing, sipping from glasses of spiced rum, under falling cinder, and orange/ red lights.*

GIOTTO. *Looking down at his folded hands.* Even if I perish by inhaling the sulphurs I'll be illuminant in defeat. I've felt I've escaped the lists, Mr. Locato. They're cold and brazen, and until now I've always sought the safety of lists.

LOCATO. *Staring at* GIOTTO *intently.* So you've come to Monserrat as some form of liberty, some test of nerves to photograph extinction.

GIOTTO. No, Mr. Locato, I've not come here as an acrobat or a phantom, or a burst of ulterior motives.

LOCATO. *Still staring at* GIOTTO. So what is your commitment to photography. What about its chronicles, its roving insular mass? I'm asking, are you committed to its phantoms?

GIOTTO. *Sitting up in his chair, an incredulous look on his face.* How can you hold this against me? I've come here to gain trust in who I am, yet you fault me…

LOCATO. *A measured tone in his voice.* You want to take great pictures?

GIOTTO. Yes.

LOCATO. *Leaning forward.* Where's the evidence, the concrete value?

GIOTTO. *Demonstratively holds up a folder.* So you're dismissing everything that I've shown you. Everything that's brought me to this moment!

LOCATO. It's not the photographs...

GIOTTO. *Almost feverish.* Then what are you saying?

LOCATO. *Leaning back in his chair.* It's the invisible scale. There's no lightning in your approach.

GIOTTO. How could the technique be bad.

LOCATO. That's precisely the point. There's no poetic complexity.

GIOTTO. *Leaning forward.* But you fail to realize I set my subjects, I draw the mold, I defeat intrusions.

    Pause.

Pulling out a photograph and excitedly pointing to it.

Look, look. The little girl on the swing. I've caught her at an apogee, her dress is naturally blended with the Sun.

LOCATO. I can tell you've looked at Meatyard's work, at some Minor White.

GIOTTO. *Anxiously.* Yes, yes...

LOCATO. But where's the nerves, the brilliance.

GIOTTO. *Slight anger.* You've got no objectivity.

Pause.

Slightly calmer. I've come here to see you, to work on a personal mission.

Puts the photograph back in the folder. Untenses his shoulders. Takes a sip of rum. Gains a more natural sitting position.

LOCATO. I'm no authority. I simply listen to my insides speak. Then the intuition rises.

GIOTTO *gets up. Begins walking in circles around the table.*

GIOTTO. You mean the photograph gives this to you.

LOCATO. Yes, the photograph.

Pause.

What Cartier-Bresson says it's true. The photograph, not you taking the photograph.

GIOTTO *circling more rapidly. See, you're doing what you accuse me of doing—quoting theory.*

LOCATO. *Calmly.* I'm no authority, Giotto.

GIOTTO. *Slowing his pace.* What are you saying then.

LOCATO. I'm always looking into the spotless.

GIOTTO. I've seen your photographs, those mosaics of Borneo, those x-ray shapes like something from Saturn.

LOCATO *begins sipping rum, while looking at the slowly pacing* GIOTTO *in a searching manner.*

LOCATO. So they're magnets, and now you surround me with your pernicious ozone, and follow me, and swallow up my poetic guitars.

GIOTTO. The photographs you took in Lisbon…

LOCATO. The guitars were electric, I simply responded. Nothing was planned.

GIOTTO. I know, I know.

    A sudden rumbling. The table shakes violently. Cinders fall through the lightning. GIOTTO *sits. Both begin looking out of the window. Rumbling quickly quiets.*

LOCATO. So you want to take the last harried purview of Plymouth.

GIOTTO. Yes, that's what I came here for. To get at absolute response.

LOCATO. So I'm the dragon who'll open your doors to discovery.

GIOTTO. I didn't say that.

LOCATO. *In a slightly raised voice.* Then why did you come to Monserrat?

    Pause.

I'll answer myself. Because you wanted to take advantage. You've done nothing but betray yourself.

GIOTTO. So you think I'm threatening you. That I've come here to take away your supremacy.

LOCATO. All you're here to do is follow.

GIOTTO. You're not the person I thought you'd be.

LOCATO. See, you're supercilious, arrogant.

GIOTTO. *Suddenly standing, anger in his voice.* You're slandering Locato.

LOCATO. You claim originality. Now you've come here just to leech me, to wrangle from me the instantaneous. All you want is a cut and dried magic.

    Pause.

Why don't you leave GIOTTO and go back to New York. Start from the bottom. Right now all you seem to do is drift like algae or plankton. You haven't located the burning within.

Stands up, pointing at his chest.

I took years to empty myself, to feel loss, to re-ignite the tornado within.

GIOTTO. But...

LOCATO. No, listen Giotto. You haven't obscured the Sun in your fingers letting it heal by means of spontaneous persecution.

GIOTTO. I've lived...

LOCATO. No, you have not lived.

Pause

Directs GIOTTO *to assume his former setting position.*

Quantity is not a factor at this level. Just because one does things…

GIOTTO. I agree. Living is nothing but doing. It's alacrity, it's burning, it's sacrificing through essence.

LOCATO. *Sitting down in his chair.* It's theory, Giotto, it's theory. You can't deny that. I'm adamant because you've intruded. You knew I left New Mexico three weeks ago and now you arrive just to leech me of…

GIOTTO. You have powers…

LOCATO. *Leaning forwards on his elbows.* So admit that you leech me, that you have no intent of actually perishing from the sulphurs.

Now sitting up in his chair.

This is not academic grammar, Giotto. It takes time and one must mine all the instants of time.

Pause.

We're playing with the caldera of death.

GIOTTO. So if I tell you I'm suspended…

LOCATO. The leap, Giotto, the leap.

GIOTTO. What do you mean?

LOCATO. Paul Strand spoke of his apprentice years as partaking of a sum of motions no less than a decade.

    Pause.

I'm telling you, everything burns from the inside out. The senses burn and are destroyed, only to re-arise in an upper condensation of purity. This is how poetry ignites.

GIOTTO. *Somewhat dismayed.* I respect you Mr. Locato, but when you say that my pictures are culpable artifacts...

LOCATO. *Leaning back in his chair.* I never said they were culpable artifacts...

GIOTTO. You said...

LOCATO. *Sitting up, more animated.* What I said, and what I'm saying is that the primal need occur, that it electrify beyond its own means, so that the viewer is fused on first seeing.

GIOTTO. But you're throwing ciphers at me, psychic trapezes.

LOCATO. *Again, leaning forwards in his chair.* Life transmutes by torment, by plagues which amass in one's solar introversion.

GIOTTO. *A mixture of hurt and anger in his voice.* So by your assessment I've come to Monserrat for nothing.

LOCATO. You have privilege, Giotto. How do I know that your present concern is not ignited by whims. How do I know that I send you into the eerie locales of explosion that you won't panic, that you won't be overcome by the inoperable?

GIOTTO. By the fact that I'm here. Who else has appeared, who else has cared that Raphael Locato would appear in Monserrat to shoot his "Philosophical Premonitions."

LOCATO. Others knew.

GIOTTO. Yes, but have they appeared.

Pause.

Rumbling noises occur. Particles of ash begin blowing across the stage. GIOTTO *begins looking askance. A hesitant tone to his voice.*

I wanted to meet you under these conditions, under the truth of this naked friction.

LOCATO. An idealism, Giotto.

GIOTTO. No, Mr. Locato, it's my first visibility, it's my first stance in the kingdom.

LOCATO. I picked up my first camaeram when I was not much older than you are right now. Years of irregular eating and wandering, cold, odd working life, without the company of women.

Gets up and start walking in circles without breaking his speech.

I had no vocation, my birth mother had no interest in my existence, the remaining family was all dead or missing. I shot rooftops and urban settings. I felt invaded, Giotto, invaded. I could go days and days without eating or sleeping. So everything I touched was complexity, everything I thought was distilled. I knew a Mr. Vincent and he would help me by letting me share his dark room. And I would always talk to myself, I would always hypnotize my own bodily thirst with anger.

GIOTTO. Why do you regale me with biography, why do you give me guilt to decipher.

   Pause.

Stands up and faces LOCATO *angrily pulling pictures from his folder.*

LOCATO. *Semi-defensive.* I'm not accusing you.

GIOTTO. But you've said it. That I'm here to steal your secrets, that I'm here to infect your concentration with harassment.

   Pause.

Both men stare at one another in silence.

GIOTTO. *Slowly speaking.* I am not here to implicate myself, or to eclipse any heat that you might combine.

LOCATO. You come to me with this pointless super-imposition. It's this penultimate moment with this void alive inside me, ready to attempt my sensitive ascent into the streets.

   Pause.

Backing away slowly. And here I'm confronted by a lateral specter.

GIOTTO. *Moving forward with intensity in his voice.* So I'm a specter who threatens the aggrandized old leader.

LOCATO. *Angrily shaking his head.* Stop it, Giotto, stop it. You're turning me raw, and when my insides boil…

Pause.

Shouting. I want you out! I want whatever you aspire to do dispersed in a million litres!

GIOTTO. *With a false uneasy laugh.* So you want to burn salt and brandy in my coffin, to…

LOCATO. Stop speaking!

LOCATO *moves threateningly towards* GIOTTO, *as the table and chairs begin shaking, the lights begin flickering on and off, as the stage goes black.*

ACT TWO

LOCATO standing over a shaken GIOTTO.

LOCATO. *Emphatically.* Do you see what it's like to exist beside the walls of volcanoes.

    Pause.

Do you see, Giotto. You've created a pre-maturity and now it gnaws you.

GIOTTO. *Getting up slowly dusting himself off.* So what do you want me to do, re-invent my momentum by means of my own suppression?

LOCATO. But you haven't faced sustained resistance; the snipping, the ridicue, the barrers of doubt.

    Pause.

Taking a deep breath. One must invent psychic water for oneself. No solipsism, no chronic self-conniving.

GIOTTO. *Looking up at LOCATO while now sitting.*

GIOTTO. But you deny me my first combat. I've come here to shoot...

LOCATO. You'll blur the moment. All the instincts have got to flow and rivet. Then what you shoot becomes instantaneous, burning. Take the painting of Joan Miro it respirates within the sum of the magnetic.

GIOTTO. If I ask you how my stamina can extend, how my eye can reciprocate discomfort, you'll accuse me of sabotage. You'll say...

78

LOCATO. I'm not a school, Giotto. I've come to Monserrat to conjoin with premonition, to somehow document the primeval.

GIOTTO. To slash at a ravine of nickel.

LOCATO. It's like an asteroid, Giotto, an old primogeniture as dust.

GIOTTO. So the volcano as ground, and its fumes like the power of a testing mirage.

LOCATO. A mirage yes, but a mirage strengthened by its threat against the total anatomy, against the upright beasts that we are.

GIOTTO. So what concerns you are the powers which immobilize...

LOCATO. *Consternation on his face.* No Giotto, the flickering, the tension.

   A blast of cinders blows across the stage forcing both men to turn their heads form one another with violent coughing. LOCATO *begins holding his hand to his mouth attempting to speak again.*

People are leaving in droves, Giotto; can't you feel the mortality. *Still hoarse.* There may be only days left to shoot. The Sun seems ruined.

GIOTTO *begins to squirm in his chair. Then begins to nervously pace.*

Voice clearing. You came with a pre-set condition Giotto, that you would burst into photography in the wake of Monserrat. To you, it's an apocalyptic equation. The volcano and Locato, the volcano and Monserrat. And I know that you know that I know this.

GIOTTO. I see, I see...

LOCATO. *Sitting now, a riveting stare at* GIOTTO. No you don't

79

see. All you see is an extension of your name. Now you can see that the flux of imitations creates seizures, creates the drying up of vision. Of course this makes you suffer.

GIOTTO *stops his pacing and begins to waver near the window.*

GIOTTO. *In a slightly strained voice.* I can't agree with your outcome, Mr. Locato. I know I'm not safe, I know that I'm bartering with frenzy, with this sudden x-ray roulette. *As if confessing.* I agree that lists are like oblong suns always attempting to bridge the mind with the incalculable.

GIOTTO *begins slightly wringing his hands, returning to his chair to finger his rum glass.*

LOCATO. Yet you continue to mimic me, Giotto. You think that if you die, you'll somehow re-arise and continue to relish a posthumous bravery. *Tensely leaning back in his chair.* I'm saying that your extremity is not organic, it can't incorporate its own debility.

GIOTTO. Yet for all your superiority we'll both die as double heretics under a fulgurant mental wool.

LOCATO. *Leaning forwards, elbows on table.* You've never been hounded, or been forced to create under duress. *Rolling up his sleeve on his left arm.* You see these marks, gas from a sulphur volcano. I followed the workers who harvested sulphur in Java. It was a precedent for me. It's the minimum reason I've come to Monserrat.

GIOTTO. *In a lowered voice.* You've experienced certain forms of hell.

LOCATO. To know the threat from sudden liquidation. I feel as though I'm a scholar of intensity. It's as though I've summoned mirrors into my eyes, naturally connected the dialectics of the heart.

As the photographer Kikuji Kawada has stated, "I seek for analogical power," I seek for "enlargement of consciousness."

Pause.

Do you know his series called "Los Capriccios," or the auguries of Luis Gonzalez Palma, or Kozo Miyoshi when he encounters "giant paper lanterns like planets at dusk." Or the "Photo Sessesionists," or Ikko Narahara when he speaks of photography being "cryptic," being of "intuition and destiny."

GIOTTO. You inundate, Locato, you inundate!

LOCATO. I'm not here to make up preceptorial dossiers, or sculpt vertigos in the aura. But I think of the "Natural Buildings" of Volkhard Hofer, or the "Sand Relief" of Keld Helmer-Peterson. What of Cravo Neto, of Ashvin Mehta who says that the "elements form limbs of the formless."

GIOTTO. So you consider me to be the naïve gondolier, the one who conducts by blind disparity.

LOCATO. Right now you're looking for a stationary myth, for an apocalyptic circle. Look at the apocalyptic light in the Czech photographer, I think Rajzik is his name.

Again, the table begins shaking. Both men look up, quickly shielding their eyes from dust that falls from the ceiling. GIOTTO quickly dusts himself off.

81

GIOTTO. You lower yourself, Mr. Locato, you take advantage of all these people who you know.

LOCATO. *Voice raising.* No, Giotto, they are not just people, understand that. If I speak of Ferdinando Scianna, or of Miguel Rio Branco, it is not that I have wafted through various texts in museums, or focused on scholarly mayhem just to exhaust my own blood. No, No, absolutely not. It's as Rio Branco has stated, "having a map of humanity" with "all the precariousness and uncertainly of existence."

GIOTTO. *Attempting to raise up in his chair.* But everything in your voice suggests an imperial kindling, a kind of overview which mocks me.

LOCATO. The Czech, Jan Sagl, know him. His "images within images," the questions he continues to pose.

GIOTTO. So you want to grill me on august definitives.

LOCATO. The abat-jour, the condition of the abaxial, of dioterics, of wayward focusing metals.

GIOTTO. *Quietly, head partially buried in his hands.* Stop, Mr. Locato, you're hurting me, you're surrounding me with your old intellectual bulimias.

Lights begin to flicker. Ash begins falling. The men seem frozen.

ACT THREE

GIOTTO *upon uncovering his eyes, finds* LOCATO *shooting non-stop at the shapes of the falling cinders.* GIOTTO, *startled, looking back and forth between the cinders and* LOCATO. LOCATO *returns to his chair*

LOCATO. A contact occurred. *Starts and stops coughing almost immediately.*

> *Pause.*

The cinders that fell were lyrically enthralling. One reacts. One simply reacts.

GIOTTO. But it's different for each person.

LOCATO. Images rivet Giotto, they rivet. A power leaps out from life and obliterates hesitation.

> *Standing up again.*

Then you have the power of superior ground, where an instinctive sun blazes, then the self-taught and the carious combine.

GIOTTO. *Incredulous.* The carious?

LOCATO. Yes, the carious. You have to see how the carious respirates with the infinite.

GIOTTO. You confuse me.

> *Begins drumming the table with a devil's tattoo.*

LOCATO. Volcanoes, uncleansed social confusions, habituations enciphered.

GIOTTO. I understand habituation, but I know its torrents shift…

LOCATO. But always within an axial cryptography.

Pauses looking into Giotto's eyes with a philosophical stare.

When you look at the scapes of Ashvin Mehta, it is a motion which transcends motion, which transmutes interior gravity.

Pause.

Habituation goes blank, and then one floats onto another plane of seeing.

The lights begin continuous flickering. Cinder continues falling and becomes more pervasive LOCATO begins coughing while remaining focused on the now standing GIOTTO.

GIOTTO. But you imply that I am already one of the ruined. That I am habituated, that I ramble outside the circle of those already enlightened. Perhaps as you suggest, the void cannot commingle with my lungs. But the more I think of it, I've suffered from the rumors you've self-sustained by means of the prejudice you've formed from my appearance. Perhaps I perplex your sonar, perhaps I've stained your Imperial foliage, your buried codes, your caliginous arcs. I don't condemn you, I do not scorch your movement, I have no regard for the cyclical rot of movement, I have no regard for the cyclical rot of fame. *Emphasizing with his right hand.* You attribute to me conduct of great jeopardy, of being suffused by omnivorous poison, as if I were hatching plots from a sorcerous codeine foundry, as if I were capable of igniting a ruinous hemorrhage. How can I obtrude according to the hesitant, according to the unspecified. According to you I'm armed with a spiteful diplomacy, with an uneven tenor, riding inside an inverted psychic litter. As if I were some kind of demonic usurper, as if I were some ravenous kindling feeding on defeated personas.

Maybe you are right Mr. Locato, maybe I am a defective specificity.
Maybe my purest effort is in photographing shields, or creating
the illusion of monsters from a smoking yield of rags. Perhaps you
need to decide this for me. Perhaps you willfully intuit that I strive
for second most, perhaps as a pointless lepton candle, or a specious
piece of wood. If I die as one of the last few scattered in Plymouth,
I am not looking for memorials, or tributes of anathema as pity. For
me, being is not rewarded in such manner. No, Mr. Locato, being is
not rewarded in such manner. No, Mr. Locato, I am not looking for
dread as a mundane manna, or for quakes that burn as accessible salt.
For me, it feels like being a strange and unerring squid in the depths,
somehow staining uninhabitable locales, being in essence a singular
minority of evil ridding himself of the commercial variation which
you accuse me of. Mr. Locato, I have not come to Monserrat to be
plagued and psychically spat upon only because my apprenticeship
seems so strenuous. Only because I've sought to open the blinding
in me, to sustain myself across prairies of doubt, walking closed
celestial scaffolds, so as to announce in myself proto-invasion by
auroras, by dense configurations of an inward looking treatise. An
inward gaze, mind you, recent, nascent, yes, but of the character of
one who seeks venom to transmute. I can tell you Mr. Locato, I am
much above the useless neon you ascribe to my various hauntings.
Much above the branded dove in a billet. If I were from Kazakhstan
or Bangladesh you night pronounce me valid. Perhaps you would
grant me the power of summoning whales, or creating the pouring of
clouds into the over activity of my lens Of course, at present I pursue
new expansional actions, rather than shooting a spout of oil in Baku,
or shooting almendras in Galacia. *Places his left foot on his chair while
continuing to stand.* I do possess an necessitous anti-grace far above
the pecunious or of privilege. My mind simply burns, Mr. Locato, my
factors locate and trans-locate, and are destroyed and re-engendered
as power. And I've begun to understand the voices inside my residue.
Knowing this, Mr. Locato, that I have swam through molten vertigo,
and that I've drowned, and lost instants, and recorded whole fields of

85

dread, so that what I've culled from suffering, has cast each particle of sun, each drought, each avalanche of bodies, soaring as a myth. Therefore, I've come to more than one mesmeric, to more than one eruptive law, causing more than one upheaval or panic.

The rumbling having accrued throughout GIOTTO'S *monologue starts to get louder. Both men look wildly in all directions.* GIOTTO *is sweating, tense.* LOCATO *begins slowly focusing in* GIOTTO'S *direction but averting eye contact. He nervously fingers his camera, and without warning begins shooting the exhausted* GIOTTO *from spontaneous angles. He pauses after inclement barrage of shooting.*

LOCATO. So you take on your own behalf the special reasoning of treason. As if I were some monarchical emblematic, who holds the hierarchical tenor of the instant. I have not questioned you as to your presence in a rainy August Brazil, just to haunt you by forcing you to count moons in precise mathematical thickets.

Pause.

There is always the pressure to over-pronounce, Giotto. I can accept this. It sometimes lets you know that you finally exist.

GIOTTO. *Starting to circle* LOCATO. So I'm setting up Galatian rhyme schemes so that you can configure me, and create from that configuration pictures of me floating in a chariot on fire pulled by a storm of Haitian Appaloosas.

LOCATO. Again, you pontificate, you corrode.

GIOTTO. *Still circling.* Mr. Locato, with all due respect, you're protecting yourself, you create limits for yourself to be.

LOCATO. *Angry.* You create these conditions.

86

GIOTTO. You're from a tribe of scholars who memorize diamonds.

LOCATO. *Less angry but voice still intense.* So I'm an emptied captain on a schooner. Or maybe I'm a flameless subtrahend, a scribe, or perhaps a curious polyhedron.

GIOTTO. *Stopping his circling, standing directly in front of* LOCATO. Of course I respect your methodology, your boldness.

LOCATO. *Still tense.* What meth…

GIOTTO. Your methodology of danger.

> *Pause.*

And I know you'll risk death in the coming hours.

> *Pause.*

It's the defiance I concur with. The witness…

LOCATO. Now you're saturating me with opposites.

> *Pause.*

More philosophical. Let me ask you Giotto, what if Monserrat exists as a general signal, if down the road of debits there occurs a larger natural instability, and if so, Monserrat is a key to apocalyptic conditioning, and if I say that I've wrought this conditioning in my speech as velocity my action can work as genetic transference.

GIOTTO. *With furrowed brow.* You mean the break up of the atmosphere, the circuitous ozone.

LOCATO. Yes, yes, schisms. *A reflective look on his face.* It's more than just withstanding corpses, or enduring frightful noises. For instance, if these corpses, or these noises were an era.

A certain calm floods over GIOTTO.

Monserrat is the era of maximum tension. Just to agree with what has passed before can carry no concern. Perhaps I'll disappear like the poet Torma into the synthesis of phlogiston, perhaps...

GIOTTO. *Calmly.* You seemed to speak as I spoke but you portrayed me as someone hackneyed, as someone decrepit with imbalance.

LOCATO. What dominates me now is the thought of scorching lava fields, of panicked reptiles and ravens. I've though of our skeletal remains warped like a void of cinders with the halo of the void passing through us.

Pause.

Emphatic. Plymouth will no longer exist!

GIOTTO'S *previously experienced calm quickly turns to panic. He begins pacing back and forth within an imaginary square. Begins speaking to himself, staring at his hands. One senses fear seeping from his pores.*

GIOTTO. *Rapidly speaking.* It's like everything exists like a strange electrical index, like a giant electrical dust. It's condemning me. It's condemning all my previous actions. How can I exist, Mr. Locato. How can I exist!

Rumbling getting louder. Lights continuing to flicker. Ash increasing in intensity. Table and chairs moving from side to side.

LOCATO. *With a loud voice.* You've got to absent yourself, empty all your random charisma. Get over the fact that you have a enclosed existence, that you are surprise by your own non-entity, knowing the moon has opened blood in the valley of the Earth.

GIOTTO *begins sitting again while burying his head in his hands.*

GIOTTO. Perhaps if I existed in Alberta…

LOCATO *begins fiercely shooting the window with the curtains blowing in. The stage blacking out and coming into view.*

Pause.

LOCATO. *Suddenly collapsing in his chair breathing rapidly.* I have it, I have it. Even the volcano knows that I have it. I'm separate from events! My solitude has left and come back to my body, knowing that even the natural forces explode and disappear.

GIOTTO. *Pulling his head form his hands, staring blankly at* LOCATO. I feel peopled by nadirs, I don't even feel my own blood. Even poison can't distract me.

LOCATO. You're beginning to feel the obscurations.

GIOTTO. *Almost relieved.* Yes, yes.

LOCATO. You're committed to apprehension.

GIOTTO *begins looking up as if staring at the rumbling.*

GIOTTO. *Blankly.* Yes.

LOCATO. It's the philosophy which pre-figures death, which takes as its presence the raw wavering in fire.

GIOTTO. *Palpably shaking.* How do you continue to live this way?

LOCATO. There's no exterior support, Giotto. You have to change your own skin. You have to multiply and reconfigure your scales.

The room begins unprecedented shaking.

GIOTTO. *Almost screaming.* It's hellish, it's hellish. It's like an evil pulchritude.

LOCATO. *A curious joy on his face.* Somewhere across the waves, the sun is breaking, I know the Sun is breaking.

Covering his nostrils with a bandana, LOCATO *definitively grabs his bag from under the table, carefully places his camera inside, and abruptly gets up from the table, and begins backing towards the door while still staring at* GIOTTO. *A panicked* GIOTTO *watching him disappear through the doorway.*

LOCATO. *His voice fading.* Go to the north, Giotto, go to the north of Monserrat, the ash won't burn you there.

The lights begin crackling. The light goes quickly in and out of blackness. GIOTTO *blankly looks up into the ash falling downward. He then slowly buries his head in his hands once again. His body quakes. The stage goes black.*

Ignacio and Galba

A Play in Five Acts

...they're bringing the dead from the arroyo.

—Federico Garcia Lorca

Characters:
IGNACIO, Proto-poet, 38, psychologically entangled, a spectre to himself.

GALBA, Fetching in mind and body, 24, teeming with connivance and reason, half sister of Ignacio.

DELVA, Oldest sister of Ignacio, mute, animalistic, unsettlingly disheveled, mentally disabled, 33.

Place:
Northern Texas

Time:
Present era, early summer

ACT ONE

IGNACIO *staring out from a spectral veranda at a blinding sundown. His younger sister* GALBA *slowly creeps behind him with an accusatory voice.* GALBA *in a long flowing dress from the neck to the floor,* IGNACIO, *in a loose fitting shirt and pants. Both are dressed in white.*

GALBA. So you want to make yourself suffer. You want to blind yourself and turn your eyes into prisms.

IGNACIO. *Still staring into the sun.* You always seek out ways to destroy me, don't you. You want to dig up pariahs so you can say that I've destroyed myself. *Slightly turning his head towards her.* It makes you gloat doesn't it?

GALBA. How can I gloat when I see you turning page after page in the books you don't write.

> *Pause.*

You want to write like the greats. You want to shock the world like Lorca with some out of date gangrene.

IGNACIO. *Turning back towards the sun.* I'm thinking, I'm absorbing.

GALBA. *Mocking.* You're always thinking, always absorbing.

IGNACIO. So I should already have my complete works. I should be an icon of the continents.

GALBA. I'm not telling you to be God. I'm not telling you to force yourself...

IGNACIO. *A controlled anger in his voice.* You always want some kind of proof from me, even if it's just a nonsensical hook on the page.

GALBA. I mean something ignited, Ignacio, something you've poured from your spirit, something that the eyes of the world can see.

IGNACIO. *Angrily.* A product!

GALBA. No, and you know...

IGNACIO. It's the money that's been spent on my upkeep. Admit it. It's what you contend is plagiaristic upkeep.

    Pause.

If I write and publish a dozen books, then you'll find something else and chew on another portion.

GALBA. What do you mean a dozen books?

IGNACIO. One on the conundrum of botany, another on astrological séance, another on the differential weathers in the vicinity of Saturn.

    GALBA *breaking in.*

GALBA Then why don't you just irrigate the spectrums, why don't you just take its mirror from the silos' mouth and break it, and create your own verbal ammonia.

    Pause.

    Angrily grabbing his right shoulder and turning him face to face with her.

93

You have nothing to do. I sweat with Delva day in and day out trying to force her to speak again.

>*Pause.*

You don't care! All you do is sup the spectral blood from your diaries.

IGNACIO. *Voice intensifying.* You've never seen them, how do you know anything bout them.

GALBA. *Backing away for him.* I'm tired. I've lied for you, I've bought blizzards of books for you...

IGNACIO. Inspiration has no plan.

>*Pause.*

Look at the cinders of Van Gogh. Look at the echoes from the Olmecs. All they could do was gamble with existence.

GALBA. *Backing further away.* Excuses Ignacio, nothing but excuses.

IGNACIO. What are you, some kind of jealous mother lion?

GALBA. No, you are the one who's jealous. I can't see you going on like this. And us insides this manger bickering all day, searching for flecks of gold in the blood.

IGNACIO. See, now you abstract me with images, with your tornadoes of blunting.

GALBA. I'm only asking that you do what you say that you do.

IGNACIO. No, Galba, you're like an ironic old witch always pursuing

94

my inspiration as if it were a serpent to be bought or sold.

GALBA. I've lost myself over you. The inheritance is almost gone!

IGNACIO. You agitate and you agitate, and it's always about money. You're staring at my efforts like a failed growth of crops.

GALBA. *Plaintively.* I'm with you because I once loved you.

IGNACIO. *Intently staring at her.* Now you're drifting to the other extreme where you're tasting the flecks of hate, where you're enjoying my disintegration.

GALBA. I don't want to hate you. I just want to…

IGNACIO. You've given in to the cold lusts of inversion.

> GALBA *sits down in a wicker chair on the veranda agitated.* IGNACIO *moves directly over her, so that he is standing inches away from the chair.*

It's the way the Olmec in me scorches. That's our chasm, that's the reason things are holding us back,

GALBA. *Looking up in disbelief.* How can you…
IGNACIO. I've created poverty simply by my presence. You know I was prone to Delva before you came of age, and now you want to spite me, to take the inspiration from my natural engenderment.

> GALBA *regathering herself. Sitting upright in the chair.*

GALBA. So you mock me and counter-mock me because I was born at a certain time. So you want to blame Jose and Ambrosia for not co-habiting sooner. I guess then you could alter dates to your liking.

IGNACIO. So you're claiming age as your reasoning.

GALBA. You're too close. Get away.

IGNACIO. Delva and I are your purest targets.

GALBA. *Standing up.* It's not about jealousy, or blood, or money. You forget about the food that I feed you!

IGNACIO. Then why do you hound me for answers? Why do you mimic my emptiness with your mind?

GALBA. What about the Tangara Animations, I never resisted your urge to write them. The way you described them they were more than ignited bulletins, but I never saw the result.

> GALBA *Suddenly grabs his hands.* IGNACIO *averts her stare.*

You once described them as "orange and compressed jade."

IGNACIO. *Continuing to look away.* You mean the poem on The Lightning River.

GALBA. Was it ever done, did any fragments survive?

> *Backing away from* IGNACIO.

If you had continued to wander inside that poem.

> IGNACIO *retreats to the chair.*

IGNACIO. No poet gets power from his efforts. No salt, no rubies, none of the tangible composts.

GALBA. *Slightly angered.* But you do nothing but sit and listen to your dimness flare. Then you watch me suffer and ignite my doubt over and over again.

Pause.

When was the last time you made mention of Delva. Since you stopped using her...

IGNACIO. Shut up!

GALBA. No, no, you listen! You attempted her, you had her, you soured her ability to speak.

IGNACIO. You're confused.

GALBA. If she couldn't speak, she couldn't indict you, she couldn't claim you as the groveling paramour that you are.

IGNACIO *turns away from her and starts to stare at the waning sun.*

IGNACIO. What you want is equations, Galba, perfectly timed equations. Always concessions to the visible life.

GALBA. Did I say I was looking for visible result.

IGNACIO. All your actions imply it. *A more serious tone in his voice.* I'm not longer an exotic figurine you can locate with your voice. I am not an animal you can exhibit or perpetuate.

GALBA. *Half pleading, half commanding.* Turn around Ignacio, show yourself, show yourself to me.

IGNACIO. *Turning partially towards her, angrily muttering.* You see, I'm something, I'm your philosophy of absence.

GALBA. I've heard your complaining.

IGNACIO. I can feel your pressure Galba. I know and you know that there is real power in disappointment.

GALBA. *Somewhat taken aback.* It's not what I want…

IGNACIO. If I disappeared…

GALBA. So you think I want you dead.

IGNACIO. What else could it be. You know there are ways of dying without leaving the body.

GALBA. As if I had some tainted rational capacity.

IGNACIO. Because I see that you are parallel to me. That my shadow rotates around in your blood.

GALBA. I've spoiled you and you know it. I give you bread, I give you the money that festers inside you.

IGNACIO. So now I'm forced to wash myself in guilt.

GALBA. There's a problem and you know it.

IGNACIO. You're trying to personalize our differences.

GALBA. I'm related to you Ignacio.

IGNACIO. Remind me, remind me again that the color of your family strain is lighter, and that I'm the older, darker castaway.

Pause.

Now face to face with her. *Tense.* Have I finished the inventory, have I finished the declaration that you've always wanted to hear, that I'm weaker, poorer, darker.

GALBA. Stop it! Stop it!

IGNACIO. You wanted to look poetic, brave. Take the poet in, console his mentally deprived sister.

Moving even closer to her.

You felt that the sun would rise and set in you because of your curious kind of altruism. I'm the poorer relations, so the suffering that you claim...

GALBA. You make me suffer. I grant you every liberty, but all you do is respond with rum, and raving about all your projects that fail.

IGNACIO. Fail?

GALBA. What about the Olmec drama you projected, the trilogy of poetic epics, the stories to be masterminded, your collaboration with giants?

IGNACIO. Is this some kind of court? Some kinds of necromancer's inquisition?

GALBA. So you accuse me of fixation.

IGNACIO. Galba, all you want are obvious answers. I can hear what you say in between.

GALBA *begins backing away and shaking her head.*

That's what makes you vertiginous.

GALBA. You strain me to the breaking point. And now you mock me. You turn my thought around in your old and embrangled wheat.

IGNACIO *stroking his brow.*

IGNACIO. I'm trying to get at something.

GALBA. You've turned in to nothing, Ignacio. I can feel it. It's like tasting old sulphur in the mouth.

IGNACIO. How typical. I know the next word out of your mouth will be bitterness.

GALBA. So I don't have all the words. But I've never told you to write this or write this. I've never told you how to model yourself, or extract emptiness from yourself, or turn into a lake, or a suspended roof in the galaxies.

IGNACIO. So I'm the goat in the Jaguar temple. I'm the anti-luminous Lutheran.

GALBA. You turn everything I say into poison.

IGNACIO. I speak through my own symbols.

GALBA *derisively shrugs her shoulders.*

GALBA. Okay. It's an asthmatic ballet. So maybe I might want to make you play roulette with a dark Alaskan wine. Then you can rotate and rotate and rotate…

IGNACIO. You're ruse is to keep me maniacal, to try to manage my stinging whispers. It makes you feel happy.

GALBA. The trouble is, you drink all the time, you molest whores in your sleep. You know I'm right. You can't deny that you want your sperm to burn my palette. This is coming from your own blood kin.

IGNACIO. You accuse and accuse. You're always seething.

GALBA. It bothers you that I date you with youth. That all your inward schemes plummet, that your voice turns rotten inside me.

IGNACIO. When do you cease. Always trying to stun me. To give a cold performance of bile.

GALBA. *In a heightened tone.* You've brought yourself to this by flagrantly meandering.

IGNACIO. Well I guess you are the perfect engenderment of balance. Never moving away from your clutches. Trying to live at a level by getting power to seduce power.

GALBA. *Backing away.* You're deluded, Ignacio. You assume a position, which is weaker than treason.

IGNACIO. So you assume that you have power. When you use the word treason, you think you've become empress in the golden armchair, or the principle riot nurse, or the girl with the factual calculus in her midst.

GALBA. You know and I know that I've never become clear to you. You attribute things to me, which erupt from your own weakness.

IGNACIO *begins nervously pacing back and forth in front of* GALBA, *raising and lowering his head while furtively glancing at her.*

GALBA. You can't bite me, or scar me, with anything you enact.

IGNACIO. *Stopping in front of her.* So now I serenade you with spiders?

GALBA. You're hounded, Ignacio, and any action you condone must perish.

IGNACIO. So what do you want from me, Galba? Maybe one cup of good blood. Or maybe I'll paint a boat from one of my mirages. Perhaps the magic will conjunct in you and you'd seem less vicious, less frail.

GALBA. So I've taken on proportions of the royal court. Perhaps I fantasize emblems, or create rural tribulations. Or perhaps I am an animal, perhaps I'm alchemic sculpture.

IGNACIO. You gambled on me and always wanted failure from the gambling. I was exotic to you. I made the fuel inside you burn. You can say that I lured you with my fuel. And now you're the weary Galba, with less and less life to seize. Even the saints have left you in limbo.

GALBA. You know I've ceased believing, you know I don't tabulate my consequence by prayer. I was born by the grace of turbulence and I've always been prone to malefaction. You know this. Why have I provoked scandal? Why have we poured our essence on sporadic sheets? I'm not claiming any kind of resistance, or trying to define malfunction. I feel like some ambiguous reptile, sullenly cleansed by solar blood. So do I study hagiographies? Have I ruminated upon Ignatius of Antioch and his coining of the word "katholikos"? For

instance, if the church were a flotational urn, it might be bearable…
The old restrictions would bend for the less magically inclined.
The Churches' brutish decalcomania gives them succour, hope,
accommodation of mystery. Which amounts to a simple notebook
on doleful triggering urns, working on the mind with less buffeted
coloration. The common mind then becomes an accessible nuance.
For me, I've opted for bottomless mendacities, for hopeless
estrangement.

IGNACIO. Create a stillborn hagiography.

Turning to the audience.

Born INEZ PHILOPIA MENDOZA, *either July 29ᵗʰ, or April 25ᵗʰ,
of medium build, light complexioned, eyes of wayward smouldering
magnets. Her triumph, chastisement of the sun in her loins.*

GALBA. Then, am I to assume that you possess the plasma of
salvation. That you've scattered the imminence of darkness?

   IGNACIO *begins facing* GALBA, *slowly moving towards her.
He imperceptibly stops, and she unexpectedly begins circling him.*

So I'm a strange omega mother to you. Can it be agreed that I am
the idealization of entropy, as time flowing backwards, brewing
from a mound of diamonds unintelligible black rays. The result,
perhaps, a reversed magnetic insight, a differential Kelvin, an invisible
background void.

Pause.

Continuing to circle.

I can tell that your response will be to test me. To take away from my psychic cup 12 interior leeches so as to give back to me a simplified origination.

GALBA *then stops in front of* IGNACIO.

IGNACIO. I'm not seeking for blood, Galba, but what I'll call those scarred marks on saliva.

GALBA. Is this your way of teaching me in-action? Of stripping away all exhibit?

Slowing circling him again.

I don't see you building up documents with your thirst. I don't see you carrying folios of water in your hands. Maybe you're more driven by thoughts of lice in your stomach. Perhaps one day you'll speak as an untenable viper.

IGNACIO. What am I to do, create rulership in emptiness? What's my advantage, a lopsided poison tree? A monster that vomits messages from his spine?

GALBA. So am I indicating cholera, a charred river of fever?

IGNACIO. As if your blood had no error. As if your lust were virginic?

GALBA. How can the poisons blind you so strongly?

IGNACIO. *In a slightly raised voice.* Poisons? Your poisons, Galba? It's like someone staining blood on the outside panes in winter. It holds its own virulence in ice. Let me ask you, what about that Priest you know who calls himself Jonas?

GALBA. He's nothing to me.

IGNACIO. *Jealous.* Why don't you confess that he consumes you. That he wallows with you in the infernal. That you're both consumed in practical damnation.

> *Pause.*

This is not about self-justification. I could say that I've never raped or killed. Or that I've targeted jeopardy in a fellow human being.

> GALBA *now stock still listening.*

GALBA. Then when do you ever inquire about Delva? Remember, this is your own blood sister, and all you do is carry omission on your breath.

IGNACIO. *Defensively.* I do think about her.

GALBA. So does your mind burn with her image when you back away from guilt?

> GALBA *retreats to the wicker chair.*

You're hiding in failure.

> GALBA *begins slowly raising her dress so that she exposes herself to* IGNACIO.

GALBA. See, Ignacio, this is the source of what's desired.

IGNACIO. *Slightly trembling.* As if I carried two lenses in my hands.

> GALBA *continuing to expose herself.*

105

As you know I'm raising up forces for which you have no conclusion. It creates a hallucinogenic in your evil. And you've treated me…

IGNACIO. I've always treated you…

GALBA. Like what!

IGNACIO. *More stable.* You spit up corrosives. You…

GALBA. You threaten me, you hound, you litter my intelligence with your plans.

> GALBA. *Begins slowly inching down her dress.*

IGNACIO. *Shaking his head.* What you're showing me is your body as a labour of suicide.

GALBA. What I've done is blackly reduce you to the ghost that you are.

IGNACIO. Always threatening, threatening, threatening.

GALBA. No.

IGNACIO. You want to play with a cleaver while I'm sleeping.

GALBA. No.

IGNACIO. Disarm me with your womb.

GALBA. No.

IGNACIO. Blank my power out with ampersands.

GALBA. No.

IGNACIO. But I'm getting to you Galba.

GALBA. How can you get to me if all I ask you to do is describe the sun, transmute verbs, malinger over wheat.

IGNACIO. I'm not...

GALBA. *Mocking.* A student to a school marm.

IGNACIO. You test every nerve that I own.

GALBA. And you're telling me that's bad.

IGNACIO. Underneath you're ruthless.

GALBA. Does that mean I'm not living.

IGNACIO. No one said you're not living.

GALBA. So apologize.

IGNACIO. How can I tell you what you want me to tell you. You want me to copy existence and place a pattern around your head.

GALBA. It seems as though you want me to copy your existence, and...

IGNACIO. Lean on my glimmers.

GALBA. They're ruses.

IGNACIO. It's something I exist by.

107

GALBA. No. It's something you attempt that lets you know that you exist.

IGNACIO. *Laughing.* Galba, the land bird tangled up in her nostrums.

GALBA. *Completely brings her dress down and sits up in her chair.*

GALBA. *Bitterly.* Shut up Ignacio.

IGNACIO. So you can't…

GALBA. I'm a decibel that can't be heard.

IGNACIO. Then I'm walking inside your nerves, I'm building flukes inside your cells.

GALBA. What if I start starving the flukes. What if I…

IGNACIO. Then give Delva all the food. Tell her this is what Ignacio squandered. Then you can…

GALBA. Then I can convince her to disown you.

IGNACIO. Every second I see the jealousy shift inside you. Every second a stunted invicta.

GALBA. When the money runs dry, what then?

Pause.

Getting out of the chair. Pacing back and forth.

What if Delva contracted fever, I couldn't put her on the health roles.

IGNACIO. Another scenario in the mundane.

GALBA. You make me bitter by the way you stand, by the way you eat, by the way you plunge yourself in your poisonous reveries.

IGNACIO. Everything comes out now. The vultures stirring their way through your spine.

GALBA. At least vultures ground themselves. At least they understand the fact of themselves ceasing to starve.

IGNACIO. So I'm nothing but a vulture that eats you like a bloody omen.

GALBA. What if I feel burned by risk.

IGNACIO. It's not like that.

GALBA. You want to make things sound as if they clung to standard chastity.

Pause.

Go ahead, blind yourself in the standard sundown, conquer forests in your mind, dazzle the day by the night and the night by the day.

IGNACIO. Everything to you is like calligraphy or sand dunes.

GALBA. You say that because you don't think I'm capable of killing you. To you, it's a play concerning lepers, with me with a knife, flirting in a black peignoir.

109

IGNACIO. You salacious…

IGNACIO *slaps her.* GALBA *then spits at him.*

GALBA. You're going to starve you old leper. You can't even imagine how bad it's going to get.

Bells begin ringing. The stage slowly plunges into blackness.

ACT TWO

A sitting room with one dim lamp on a table stage right, parallel to a small black sofa in front of which sets a small coffee table littered with scattered keef. A chair turned backwards slightly stage right in front of the coffee table. IGNACIO standing nervously with his left foot planted on the chair's wooden sitting bottom, fidgeting, doing a devil's tattoo on his bent left knee with his left hand. GALBA sprawled on the couch, generally unkept, her white dress splotched with discolored markings, wearing old green house slippers, lasciviously licking the fingers of her left hand, and then furtively attempting to in hale the odour.

IGNACIO. You're trying to seduce me, Galba.

GALBA. It's your interpretation.

IGNACIO. Why is it my interpretation?

GALBA. Because you want me, say it, you want me.

     IGNACIO *stepping off the chair, then turning three quarters towards her.*

IGNACIO. It's nothing but blackmail, Galba. It's…

GALBA. I'm just sitting.

IGNACIO. *Fully turning towards her.* No, you're spiraling out your nets.

GALBA. *Laughing.* Give me some of your words, a ballistical chemistry, a…

     IGNACIO *seeming to get angrier and weaker at the same time.*

111

IGNACIO. You're sketching apparitions that you want me to swallow.

GALBA. Then swallow, since you do nothing but venture through stagnation.

IGNACIO. *Making a slight rocking motion fro side to side.* What made you build rain in my pores and then think in your mind that poetics can ever founder.

GALBA. So now I'm a sorceress. I condone a voudou empyrean.

IGNACIO. The jealousy just eats you alive.

GALBA. No, you're the jealous captain of the bloodline.

IGNACIO. I never claimed for myself a hypnotizing prerogative, or poured from myself a gale of advice, claiming that my mind issues unaltered diamonds.

GALBA *begins raising her legs in the air as if to taunt him.*

GALBA. *Suddenly sitting up and sneering.* You're like a cat that fails to hunt in the throes of its own hunger.

IGNACIO. *Pointing to his chest.* But I'm the one you want to tame.

GALBA. I never said I wanted to tame you. I have no needs.
She slowly sits forwards and retrieves a clump of keef from the coffee table and begins to chew. She begins quietly looking up at IGNACIO.

Jonas gave it to me.

Pause.

See how the jealousy makes you tremble.

IGNACIO. I don't know him so why should I tremble.

GALBA. *Louder.* Because you do know him. I've told you about him. Marrakesh, the keef, the argon oil.

IGNACIO. Who you talk to is whom you talk to.

      The lamp begins to flicker. A subdued moaning begins filtering into room.

GALBA. She's hungry. Why don't you feed her? I don't feel like changing her today. *Chewing more keep.* If she smells, she smells.

IGNACIO. So you accuse me of neglect, you accuse me of…

GALBA. Who else is there. Locked away like you are, sleeping with two women without let up.

      Pause.

Do you ever wash her after you've had her.

IGNACIO. You low…
GALBA. That's why my dress is stained, it's all your dried babies!

IGNACIO. *Moving closer and pointing.* Shut up!

GALBA. Then just drag her out, fondle her. Rub her privates with sleeping oil.

IGNACIO. This must be your old gullible roulette.

GALBA. Just bring her out because I can't stand touching her tonight. I know if I touch her she'll cling to me. And you know how jealous that makes you.

GALBA *suddenly leaps up from the couch and disappears.* IGNACIO *begins trembling in his rumpled clothes. He goes to the coffee table to gather some scattered keef. As he begins to chew,* GALBA *returns dragging* DELVA, *whose dressed in a stained multi-colored house coat, barefoot, slightly drooling from the mouth.* DELVA *is clinging to the left leg of* GALBA. *The latter trying to violently shake herself free.*

GALBA. *Straining and pulling.* Get something. Get something.

IGNACIO, *frozen, for a second, disappears stage right. He returns with the severed chord of a clothing iron wildly looking about.*

Hit her, just hit her!

He runs across the stage awkwardly knocking the chair out of the way. He then violently strikes DELVA *twice, and she pulls away from* GALBA *moaning.*

GALBA. *Breathing rapidly.* You did do something.

IGNACIO. What do you mean I did something.

GALBA. Rid me of her!

DELVA *begins grasping again at* GALBA *as* GALBA *begins moving parallel to* IGNACIO.

GALBA. She's your sister, tell her…

IGNACIO. Tell her what!

GALBA. She can hear…

IGNACIO. She doesn't know what I'm saying.

DELVA *begins crawling towards* IGNACIO. *He makes a start and jumps backward.*

GALBA. *Mockingly.* You're afraid of animals, aren't you.

Waving her slightly bent left arm.

A plate of snails for the tepid Monsignor.

IGNACIO. *Beginning to contract his fists.* I'll break you in…

GALBA. How can you break me if you can't lap up the filth from your own sister.

IGNACIO *tightens the cord in both his hands and attempts to garrote* GALBA. *As they struggle* DELVA *begins attempting to stand, intensely coughing, as if attempting to bring up dry vomit.* IGNACIO *drops the cord and kicks at the struggling* DELVA, *as if a beast had gotten too close.* GALBA *Then excitedly runs to the opposite side of the stage.*

Almost screaming. Pick her up and wash her!

Pause.

Staring intently at IGNACIO.

Do you want me to take matters into my own hands?

115

IGNACIO. *Backing further away.* Who can put up with your poisonous standardizing. It's like you're some old treeless salamander squirming in a morgue.

GALBA. Maybe I'm close to being dead, but I'm lucid enough to tell you to clean up the vomit. Just clean up the vomit.

IGNACIO. I'm the subordinate because the Sun has made you paler. And now you want me to dig through her intestines.

     DELVA *begins awkwardly standing, and then starts staggering around the stage, noisily slobbering, then falling on the sofa, her head having fallen over the left arm rest.*

GALBA. Go touch her, go touch her now. Every time you've had her I've cleaned her of all the dried crusting you've left on her belly.

     IGNACIO *beings to tepidly paw at* DELVA.

Touch her!

     DELVA *raises up her body and attempts to grab* IGNACIO. *She then begins to moan in an eerie, unsettling manner.* IGNACIO *steps away from the sofa.*

GALBA. When you penetrate her you never think this way, and now you want me to direct her.

     DELVA *continuing to flail at the air.*

IGNACIO. *Shaken.* So you want an exhibition.

GALBA. You're eating my nerves alive.

116

Pause.

After tonight I'd love to see both your carcasses tossed down a ravine.

> GALBA *grabs a piece of keef from the floor and begins chewing.* IGNACIO *begins furtively looking for the cord but* DELVA *is attempting to wrap it around one of his legs.*

IGNACIO. Give me the cord, Delva.

GALBA. She doesn't understand anything you're saying.

IGNACIO. Haven't I told you to keep your mouth shut.

> *Without warning,* IGNACIO *slaps* GALBA.

GALBA. *Without flinching.* Everything I've said is true. *Louder.* You know nothing, and you don't understand that you know nothing.

IGNACIO. The keef makes you bold. I'll say this; when Galba stops existing as she is, she can write her great book on what it means to deny one's own thinking.

> *Pause.*

> GALBA *now on the floor next to the prostrate* DELVA, *leaning on one knee.*

Maybe now you can think of yourself as a servant in the colonies being forced to listen to me as some Roman propaetor giving out petty commands, calling for a blue glass of rum, a scrupulous setting of plates, and three rows of black linen.

GALBA. *Looking up angrily.* Look at what you've done to us.

He kicks her. She doubles over crying, and then regathers herself, and spits at him. IGNACIO then disappears stage right and returns with a wine glass and shatters it near the huddled women.

IGNACIO. Now crawl through that. They tell me that the taste of blood is sweet.

GALBA. *Her voice breaking.* You cold, you violent…

IGNACIO *maintaining a frail state of confidence about himself.*

IGNACIO. Stop cowering.

GALBA. *Looking up.* Then pick her up! Just lick off the filth, Ignacio. What about that old jaguar's tongue always snaking down my gullet.

IGNACIO. You sound like a slaughtered cross on paper.

GALBA. How do you want me to agree. All I can sense is the swamps underneath your arms, the sunbirds drowning in your name.

IGNACIO. So now you're taking my gift from me.

GALBA *struggling to her feet.*

GALBA. I've never shown you anything written.

IGNACIO. So it's recondite.

GALBA. If you say it's recondite, it's recondite.

Pause.

You've never known me this way, Ignacio. All your knowledge blows away with the Sun.

IGNACIO. No. You want to distort the consequences, Galba.

DELVA *begins crawling around the pair as they quarrel.*

Look at her. Useless, bland, without curiosity or remorse.

IGNACIO. No. She's telepathic. She merges archaeology and remorse.

GALBA. After you kick her. After you...

IGNACIO. I've never failed her...

GALBA. Let's say that you've failed every fiber, which exists inside you.

IGNACIO. Then stop existing in me.

GALBA. So I'm commingled inside a murderer.

IGNACIO. Then where are my victims? Where is the site of my abattoir?

GALBA. They're in your neural composition.

IGNACIO. *Strained laughter.* So you want to rescue their various fates?

GALBA. *Threateningly.* Don't kick me, Ignacio.

IGNACIO. Yet you call me a dog, a plague, a dishonour?

GALBA. *Less threatening.* Let me say it another way. You're a dangerous lessening.

119

IGNACIO. What you're saying is that I'm an impact monster, I'm something…

GALBA. Look how Delva crawls around us. It's like her rotted canines are dripping.

IGNACIO. You exaggerate.

GALBA. *Pointing to* DELVA. Look at her. She's cold, she's teeming with vomit…

IGNACIO. And you have no result in this? You bear no causality, you've never authored any ruin?

GALBA. No. You've let her circle our bodies with vertigo.

> DELVA *struggles to her feet and stumbles to the sofa where she falls, and she gains an awkward sitting position. She begins absently staring at* IGNACIO.

GALBA. See, you can't stand her looking at you.

> GALBA *going over, aggressively whispering to* DELVA.

See how he treats you. See how weak he is in front of you. See how he hates to touch you with his eyes.

> GALBA *now wild with electricity, circling the sofa with a vindictive gain in her stride.*

The sound of thunder and bells engulfs the stage. The light begins actively dimming.

ACT THREE

A dimmed light composes the stage. GALBA *is putting a clean sackcloth on* DELVA. IGNACIO *is now sitting in the chair exhausted, his clothing more severely rumpled.*

GALBA. *Struggling with* DELVA'S *sackcloth.* Did I say I want you muted.

    IGNACIO *head buried in his hands. Then slowly raising his head so that he captures Galba's gaze form the corner of his eye.*

GALBA. *More and more confident.* What I say to you, you claim is reasoning. Or maybe you think I make your ice flash and turn its sound into darkness.

IGNACIO. Now you want to hound me and mimic your own abstraction.

GALBA. I could say that I'm a tribe of bickering alphas…

    She finally finishes fitting DELVA. *Again,* DELVA *renews a curious sitting position as if she were looking at the both of them.* GALBA *assumes a standing position behind the sofa.*

Laughing. You've chewed on too much vodka and keef. A scorched and gloomy lizard you are.

IGNACIO. You seem to want it this way. It's like you're trying to assassinate your own guilt.

GALBA. So I've objectified depravity.

Pause.

121

No. It seems like I'm starting to overwhelm your own grammar.

IGNACIO. You're trying to drain me.

GALBA. Maybe I am a witch. Maybe I do milk ravens.

IGNACIO. *More intent, stronger.* I can't make myself swallow your breakage. You're a blind old corpse seeking damage.

GALBA. *Shrugging her shoulders.* Defame me if you want.
Ignite him, Delva.

> *Suddenly* DELVA *begins staring wildly about. Then just as quickly begins staring at* IGNACIO. *It makes both of them uneasy.*

IGNACIO. Stop using her!

GALBA. She listens, Ignacio, all she does is listen.

IGNACIO. You've fixed her. You've fixed the smoke in the crystal that she carries.

GALBA. She's a great lotus. If it's hatred that dwells within her, it's her electrical suffering, it's her predisposition to want.

> IGNACIO *gets up and stands in front of* DELVA, *moving back and forth, using improvised hand signs to calm her down.* DELVA *slowly retreats back to stillness.*

IGNACIO. *Facing* GALBA *with* DELVA *between them.* I've never held her back. I've only given her…

GALBA. Stumbling fissures, curses. Stumbling, fissures, curses.

IGNACIO. You're looking for models, for something to assuage the nettling inside your carcass.

IGNACIO. Maybe I'm allowing you to cleanse yourself with friction.

> GALBA *suddenly exists stage left and returns with an expensive blue amphora.*

Galba, *Handing it to* DELVA. Break it if you despise all the times he's licked you.

> DELVA *blankly fondles the amphora. She begins staring wildly in all directions, neither looking at* IGNACIO *or* GALBA. *A tense silence ensures, with* IGNACIO *and* GALBA *riveted upon her presence burning like a scattered oracle.*

IGNACIO. Why do you wait for her? Why do you wait to prompt her?

GALBA. You assume prompting, and you assume that it's against you.

> *Pause.*

Persecution only stings one's self-assault.

> DELVA, *having calmed, she begins pointing in random directions with her left index finger, and without warning breaks the amphora.* IGNACIO *stands listless.* GALBA *attempts to pick up the pieces when* DELVA *suddenly springs on her back making unintelligible noises.* IGNACIO *begins to refocus himself and for a short duration gloats.*

GALBA. Get her off of me! Get her off of me!

IGNACIO. *Loudly.* She hates you. She's exploded all the rumours that you've mongered.

GALBA. Get her off me!

     IGNACIO *grabs* DELVA *by the shoulders. The stage goes black. There is struggle and moaning in the dark. When the light goes on,* DELVA *sits in the middle of the sofa, drooling, staring blankly into space.* IGNACIO *and* GALBA *stand in front of her, heaving, their white clothes stained by blood and saliva.*

This is what you've made of her. This is your interpretation.

IGNACIO. *Staring at* GALBA. My interpretation?

GALBA. Yes, your interpretation.

    Pause.

Breathing heavily. You want to linger as some charlatanic Don Juan. Now Delva has brought you her gifts from old lingering.

IGNACIO. You stay confused Galba. You roam like a legacy through a leper's tomb. You speak of fortnights and tombs in your sleep.
GALBA. If anyone should know it is you. Always trying to stir up the insatiable in me.

    Pause.

A year ago I thought it was either poignant cholera or a feast. Now…

IGNACIO. Now what. You can't stand the rutting, you can't stand…

GALBA. Then I believe that you're Delva's father.

    Pause.

Why would the family cross themselves in your presence. If it wasn't for me you'd be dead. You'd be in a freezer with tags.

GALBA *notices* DELVA *trying to chew on the shards from the broken amphora.*

Panicked. Stop her Ignacio, stop her!

IGNACIO *in trying to hastily grab the shards from her mouth, cuts himself. He pulls away from holding his hand to staunch the bleeding.* DELVA *stares blankly at the scene, while* GALBA *stares petrified as if a horrific realization had taken root.*

IGNACIO. Help me Galba, help me, because if she dies…

Looking up at GALBA.

You're going to waste, Galba. Help me!

GALBA *suddenly rushes to* DELVA *and begins putting her fingers down her throat.*

GALBA. What if she becomes spasmodic? What if her nest blackens?

IGNACIO. You want me to tell you if she'll die?

GALBA. To me, it's the utterance, which attempts to allow you to own yourself.

IGNACIO *holding the stilled* DELVA'S *head, blankly staring, a new level of absorption in his voice.*

IGNACIO. One can own a tendency, salute allegiance to dearth, specify commandments to God, drink in contaminates of soil, become

125

psychological abrasion, become a panic of rules, then the final outcome translates ruination.

DELVA *begins gasping.*

GALBA. *Frantic.* She may inwardly bleed for months. Do you want that?

The stage slowly blackens to the mumbling of voices.

ACT FOUR

DELVA *begins violently moaning.* GALBA *exits stage left and returns with a saturated towel, daubing her brow and striking her back. Traces of blood seep from her mouth.* IGNACIO *stands up and begins pacing back and forth frantically surveying the scene.*

IGNACIO. Make her vomit. She always vomits.

GALBA *stands up and confronts* IGNACIO *face to face.*

GALBA. I know you want her to live so you can enter her sex like a dog.

IGNACIO. If she dies on us...

GALBA. She's in her blood. You raped her. You confessed that you enjoyed the terror of having your member in her mouth. And now you want me to save her.

IGNACIO. If she dies...

GALBA. Then I guess you'll ask me if I want to burn up the corpse and have arrangements made at some underground crematorium. Then your diaries will boil from neglect. The disgrace will shine like anemia.

IGNACIO. Are you finished?

IGNACIO *violently grabs the towel from* GALBA *and vainly begins striking the weaker and weaker* DELVA *on the back.*

I've heard about someone in Auckland who's said that he could make corpses disappear.

127

GALBA. You weak…

IGNACIO. *Voice trembling.* When she dies…

GALBA. Then I'll formally accuse you of rape and you'll have no chatter to sustain you. Those old conflicts you've accrued, those drunken mongrels you used to stumble with. Where are they now, Ignacio, where are they now when you need them to embrace you?

IGNACIO. Stay away from the phone.

GALBA. She's dying.

IGNACIO. Stay away…

 The stage goes black and when the light slowly returns, IGNACIO *is holding a knife in his right hand, while trying to clear his eyes with his left. Seeing* GALBA *in triplicate he jabs the knife in the air trying to attack her, with her all the while mocking him with rapacious laughter. The stage blackens again, and* GALBA *begins speaking in triplicate. When the light reappears he attempts to turn the knife on himself and fails. He throws his knife in a corner and runs over to the lifeless* DELVA.

Wake up, crawl, I can take you to the mountains and leave you alone. You can stop bleeding. I'll garner enough money for eating. You can change gowns by the hour. I'll get women to dress you. You will live and the Sun will eat through you every day, all the phantoms will leave your body, then the botched shelters, the sudden unicorn diseases will all vanish Delva. All gone away, just the two of us in the mountains under the Sun. There'll be sturgeon and animals and we can swim inside a recluse lake. I'll soak your beak in argon oil, I won't chatter or pontificate, I won't leave you scattered with needles in your arms, even as I wear a tonnage of brine on my shoulders. We'll be small again, we'll have Ambrosia cook dates for us and mingle bread with the stones. I can't tell you how better things will be, and we'll be separate and original and fresh to ourselves. On days when the sun burns green I'll take an Iguana and slice it, and we can study the organs and make drawings and do all the things, which allows the surmounting of modesty. We can cultivate grass from the rocks, and I can show you the certificates from the things I've made. And every problem that will contain us will de-voice itself, will astound us with its absence through in-variety, letting us step through the veil of deadly verbal otters.

Now kneeling beside DELVA, *turning her bloody face towards him.*

Do you agree, Delva, can we start time over again, can we wait and start again, can the impact be won,? I know you understand me Delva. I can speak, and you can hear me, and I know you hear me, because I've pulled you back from the heat of not hearing, because in an hour you'll mumble, in three days you'll ambulate, and day after day you'll be the photographic Delva, the energetic Delva, extracting dice from your own acres.

He shakes the corpse again and so as to prove himself real. GALBA'S *voice begins to echo.*

GALBA. Now you want to exist, now you want to newly shift yourself.

IGNACIO *looking up frightened. Then the chair seems to cast* GALBA'S *voice.*

You want yourself shifted, the hell of your radiance shifted.

The latter phrase repeats and repeats as he grabs DELVA'S *corpse almost drunkenly.*

Pause.

GALBA *then appears in triplicate telling him to ignite himself upon command of the will of* DELVA.

GALBA. *Her mingled voice whispering.* The pyre Ignacio, the life of your body is the pyre.

GALBA *suddenly appears again.*

GALBA. She's dead, Ignacio. You've finally squandered her body. Whatever you say all your assonance exists in pitchforks, in the herbs one tangles in a letter through poison.

Pause.

At least drag her where her head's not showing.

IGNACIO. *Angrily.* As if you didn't crave her, as if you didn't seek to have her body in your clutches.

GALBA. The law knows I'm separate from you. I took you in because your body had turned ragged, because…

IGNACIO. Make yourself the victim. With the gist of your thinking you'd take a magical ocelot and brand him.

GALBA. Am I to take it that you're the magical ocelot?

IGNACIO. There's no position for argument.

GALBA. Look, your sister bled to death. We have no way of burning her, or draining the blood, or chopping the corpse into pieces.

IGNACIO. *Frantic.* Then how are we not drowned? How are we not infected by her blood?

GALBA. Drag her away. Drag her away.

Pause.

As far as I'm concerned, neither one of you has ever existed.

IGNACIO. Now you make yourself the priority figure, the one who can express her duplicity as transcendence.

GALBA. So I'm the blame. I'm the one who impaired your sister. I'm the one who slipped a clutch of cobras into her feces.

IGNACIO. Yes, yes.

GALBA. Let's be practical Ignacio. I may have friends who can take care of the body, but you'll pay Ignacio, you'll pay.

IGNACIO *frantically returns to the corpse and kicks it three times. Then very quickly drags it from view. He returns to face* GALBA *running his hands through his hair.*

IGNACIO. I didn't kill her. I didn't touch her. She ate the glass.

GALBA. You did nothing to stop her.

IGNACIO. You created the jealousy. You created the sand traps, the monstrous bluntings.

GALBA. No Ignacio. You were destitute and you had no qualms about me. Am I not right? Your half of the family was dead, and you had no need of Delva. I gave you the freedom to write, to ignite the lands with oxygen, yet all you've done is entangle yourself with dread.

IGNACIO. A benefactress who rots in the charnal house, who scorches the very cup of her own blindness.

GALBA. She's your sister, with your blood, with your features.

IGNACIO. As if you weren't entangled.

GALBA. Then I'll light up a lantern and carry a bowl of her blood onto the boulevards.

IGNACIO. Have you finished your Caucasian sonnets?

Pause.

Arms akimbo. You take two darkened Olmec waifs and play at being the conqueress on high.

GALBA. So I'm holding racial daggers at your throat.

IGNACIO. I equate bodies with history.

GALBA. No. You claim politics over bodies. I've heard you claiming to Delva that I've woven a fatal piece of taffeta.

IGNACIO. Of course I aggravate you. I could just as well respond with the injunction, kidnapper, or murderess.

GALBA. But Ignacio, not navigating for yourself. At least give hellishness a name.

IGNACIO. *Mockingly.* Is this your disquisition on chaos, on your thermal registration on the nameless. *Clapping.* Bravo! Bravo!

GALBA. Listen. What will happen when she starts to smell, when her body breaks apart and reeks?

Pause.

Ignacio, Delva is not living. She's no longer the person you've limited to family trauma. She's no longer the malfunctioning artery in the system.

IGNACIO. Then who do you know?

GALBA. What do you mean, who do I know?

IGNACIO. The body. The disposal of the body.

GALBA. Now you need my electricity.

IGNACIO. You're the one who mentioned disposal. Now you're acting as if I'm trying to pose as an indefinite demon. As if I was both monstrous and Chaldean.

GALBA *begins pointing demonstratively in the direction of the corpse.*

GALBA. Look, Ignacio. Look at the outcome you've driven me to. It would do you if I put Delva in a cart and plunged it down a cliff.

Pause.

At least cover her. At least allow her to vanish.

The stage suddenly goes black. There is rustling and movement. When the light dimly reasserts itself, IGNACIO *is rapidly moving towards the no longer visible corpse with a shroud. He begins walking towards* GALBA, *crestfallen.*

She suffered, Ignacio, she suffered. The trauma, the shocks, the rapes, the hunger.

IGNACIO. I never brutalized…

GALBA. What do you mean never brutalized. Always trying to defend your irrelevant mean.

 IGNACIO. Me! It's you. Always wanting to turn the rainbows black.

GALBA. So I'm author of the incest chamber. I've carved a picture of photinos and made you suddenly glisten.

IGNACIO. Then bury her in a ditch of salt.

GALBA. You are a rotten…

       IGNACIO *moves threateningly towards* GALBA. GALBA *just as quickly circles away from him.*

If you come any closer your throat is mine.

    Pause.

Don't you know I'm even supporting you in death. I've given freely. Even though you are a literary ghost, I've supported. And I don't have to say it with a knife in my fingers. All I can say is that all the water in you is gone, every figment seems collapsed.

IGNACIO. It's Galba's bouquet of thorns.

GALBA. Ignacio's great maxim of duress. It's just tedious, you just consume me with the tedious.

IGNACIO. This house is like an old lake in a brothel.
GALBA. Then you're the architect of the brothel.

IGNACIO. You are the female Judas who wants to spy on the dead.

GALBA. I could plagiarize your steps, or mimic your roots by making your voice sweep all the jade from the oceans.

IGNACIO. So now I'm erratic...

GALBA. No, I'm simply pointing lenses at your soil.

Light slowly fades to the sound of agitated whispers.

ACT FIVE

GALBA *is circling the room.* IGNACIO *sits erect on the sofa.*

GALBA *pointing at* IGNACIO. That's where you always left her. That's where I'd always retrieve her, and wash her, only to have her be reclaimed by your member. Deny it IGNACIO. Deny last April 25th. Deny those couplings in the Orchid Room, as if I had no inkling.

IGNACIO. *Attempting to laugh.* I get it. You're jealous of Delva. Always making those rotted scenarios of intrigue and pride. Ah, the great scenarios of intrigue and pride. Ah, the great Ereshkigal, the domestically reduced Ereshkigal.

Pause.

Wishing in each of your twelve personas, as bodies on a boat floating in the Tigris, writhing with inflamed vulvas, throwing aromatic dice on the prow.

GALBA. You lie and vouch with shredded wood. That's why your family is all dead. That's why the demons have you marked.

IGNACIO. *Looking squarely at* GALBA. Then bury her in the ozone and stop thinking!

GALBA. The great poet that you are. The old prestidigitator who finally bears witness.

IGNACIO. Is that all you can say.

IGNACIO *suddenly stands and begins inching towards* GALBA *so as to cut off her motion.*

Now you want to ignite another murder.

GALBA. *Trying to deflect his gaze.* You have to stop Ignacio, you have to stop.

GALBA *bewildered, drops to one knee claimed by partial shadow. Suddenly* IGNACIO *is lit by a green funnel of light.*

IGNACIO. You've never understood gestation, Galba. Your nature disdains conjoinment. This is why I'm connected to magicians. My ghosts are from Huasteca. Therefore I'm juggling the jaguar spectrums. It's a fresh scale of laws. All you give are colossal salaams to Madrid. For myself I can say that I'm moving through the throes of patience and death. Long before Christ, I ate the blood from jaguar's tables, I long predated Swedenborg with his visions of the afterlife. Of stinging mystical assaults, it seems that all your poison can do is lurk between walls. Your isolated mongering will make you pay for this. Listen to me Galba, I know you desire to flay yourself, to psychically tie yourself to a sunken x-ray post subjecting yourself to intellectual capture. How can any of their planning techniques compare to crops of pure starlight? You can't answer me Galba, you can't look at my surface obscurities and give a chronicle with your European gestures in advance. In this sense you can offer no moral apology excusing yourself according to inadvertent flaw. Try gazing in yourself according to he tenets, which dwell in darkened sea ravines, according to trenchant hypnotizing focus. What you seem to never understand is that circulation exits in emptiness. Between auroras, in sudden star eclipses, which allows one to reconnoiter the green sun in oneself. It exists as dictation, as something, as an unbearable fascination, which burns as if the skin were inflamed with grammatical hives. Then one can rise above the dialectics of the treacherous, above the uncleansed sonar, which rebounds from the limits of a morbific tarantula pot. One then decreases denseness. Do you hear me, Galba, do you know, and do you just this once understand that I am not regaling you with wool, or attempting to awaken in you a crude didactic lesson. By living you will see that I enact a region of proof, that I have freed myself from limit, which conjoins a kind of action according to terminal scale. What I say to Galba, soars inside itself according to an ominous transitional balance. This is not to say that I've subscribed to a treatise on beasts. That I dwell in the vacant room of a leper. One can never say this, Galba. But as an alchemist of the arts, I take the seeming road of ruin, I take the road of the ashen sun, and confabulate, and open the doors seemingly marked by terrifying flaw. So if you accuse me of mundane intoxicants, if you seek to frame me according to banter in the alehouse, you are missing you are lost and cast through free space. Because I am consumed by an essence which brews itself in torment, which respires by incalculable menace. I am this person Galba, I am this vapourous element who seemingly destroys. I am not asking for laws to bend, or for commandments to re-triangulate density. I've taken into my substance an arc of Nubian scarabs, so that they hover in my aura, allowing me to gaze far beyond my destinal boundary. True, guilt has wracked my organs, the silver in me has sometimes blackened, but I've always mined from my failing toxicity new powers. I've kept breathing, I've kept existing, and I've been told in these latter few moments that Delva has fully awakened after death. I've heard an oracle from San Lorenzo telling me that Delva is alive, that she's disembarked at Tanis, that she's a pure Phoenician Goddess. You see Galba, now I've truly appeared, and now I can consume your curious cortical room. Perhaps I frighten you in this state, but so be it. Roam, conjoin yourself like Delva, be like glass or wind. In your present state you can never contend that a prairie is real, or if orogeny exists as dust across the eye. Because I must be ruthless, Galba. Because you've taunted me, because you've hounded me, stamping my sigil as weakness, you've fallen to the level of stark confessor's slaughter. Tell them that I've taken my whole life to send signals in this manner, tell them that the Euro-Mandarin has been broken. I, who have posed to you as an obscure novice evolved from Veracruz, part Carib and part maroon, being an essential configuration from The Republic of Palmares. I am Veracruz and

Palmares via psychic volcano, via 1051 B.C. For instance, Delva is now eating birds in her grave. She is cloudless in her mind with no need to cast scorn. When she starts to stir the world she will clean you, she will carry you away from this life, with all your tactile remembrance floating between Tanis and La Venta. Yes Galba, you'll be acrobatic mongrel, you'll be a claw of sands who juggles away instants. I'm summoning her from Rio Balsas to remind you, Galba, that the world has now turned, that the Sun no longer afflicts itself with bondage. As of now you are freed from capricious rulings, from seeming family contestations. The cart and the ravine can no longer claim you. Yet the family is not dead, it only suffers from interregnums. But because Jose and Ambrosia are stricken, you have no cause to waver Galba. You have no need to luxuriate in hanging. Yet their death is not endless. I'm addressing you now as unfixed destinal schema. Spain is now burnt like the Olmec women from Xochipala. You will vomit up the robberies of Cortez, you will then see the first Egyptian cross at La Venta, called by the beings of the kingdom Tonacaquahuitl. Then you will embalm the corrupted labours, which issues from Judea. You will annul the gold of the Western saviours. I now pronounce you the concubine of challenge.

He snaps his fingers, the green light disappears, the stage goes black, then just as quickly a flickering dim yellow light reappears.

GALBA *a mixture of fright and defiance, slowly rises from her kneeling positions and uneasily approaches* IGNACIO *with a knife. As she does so* DELVA *begins awkwardly stirring beneath her shroud, moaning and noisily turning beneath the shroud.* GALBA *looks sidelong at* DELVA.

She then begins darting in different directions across the stage. IGNACIO *begins ghoulishly laughing. The lights dim. A faint sound of Tibetan nuns chanting.*

139

NOTE ON THE AUTHOR

In the tradition of Sun Ra and Aime Cesaire, Will Alexander's poetry combines the surreal with an extra-terrestrial perspective on the relation of humans to mind and the cosmic environment. His perspective emerges from Africa and the Earth's trans-oceanic rim. He is also a poet, essayist, novelist, philosopher, visual artist, as well as playwright. His myriad books include *Vertical Rainbow Climber* (1987), *Asia & Haiti* (1995), *Above the Human Nerve Domain* (1998), *Towards the Primeval Lightining Field* (1999), *Exobiology as Goddess* (2004), *Sunrise in Armageddon* (2006), and *The Sri Lankan Loxodrome* (2009). A Whiting Fellow, a California Arts Council Fellow, and a PEN Oakland National Book Award recipient, Will Alexander lives and works in Los Angeles.

About Chax Press

Chax Press was founded in 1984 as a creator of handmade fine arts editions of literature, often with an inventive and playful sense of how the book arts might interact with innovative writing. Beginning in 1990 the press started to publish works in trade paperback editions, such as the current book. We currently occupy studio space, shared with the painter Cynthia Miller, in the Small Planet Bakery building at the north side of downtown Tucson, Arizona. Recent books by Alice Notley, Barbara Henning, Charles Bernstein, Anne Waldman, Linh Dinh, Tenney Nathanson, Robert Mittenthal, Samuel Ace, Maureen Seaton, David Miller, Anne Waldman, Eileen Myles, and many more, may be found on our web site at *chax.org*.

Chax Press projects are supported by the Tucson Pima Arts Council, by the Arizona Commission on the Arts (with funding from the State of Arizona and the National Endowment for the Arts), by The Southwestern Foundation, and by many individual donors who keep us at work at the edges of contemporary literature through their generosity, friendship, and good spirits.

This book is set in Bulmer with some titling in Herman Zapf's Optima typeface and some in Trajan of varying sizes.

Book design by Charles Alexander. Cover art by Will Alexander.

TUCSON PIMA
ARTS
COUNCIL

Arizona
Commission
on the Arts

NATIONAL
ENDOWMENT
FOR THE ARTS